**GEIER
LIBRARY**
BERKSHIRE SCHOOL

❧

IRENE V. MCDONALD
COLLECTION

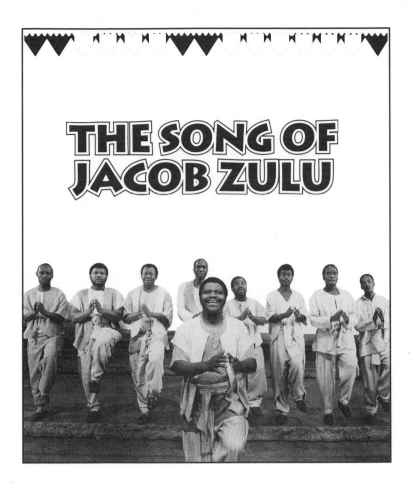

THE SONG OF JACOB ZULU

Tug Yourgrau

Photographs by Jack Mitchell

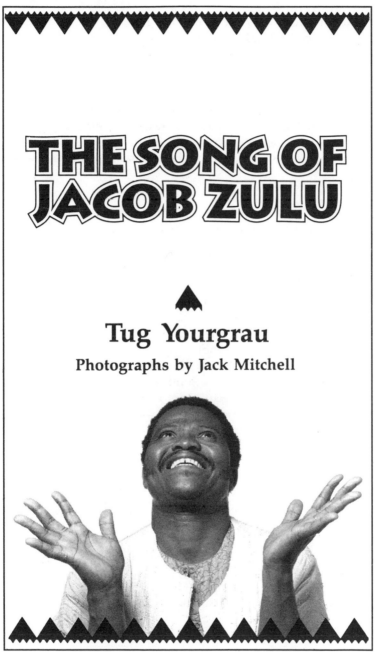

Arcade Publishing • New York

Text copyright © 1993 by Tug Yourgrau
Song lyrics copyright © 1993 by Tug Yourgrau and
Ladysmith Black Mambazo
Photographs copyright © 1993 by Jack Mitchell

All rights reserved. No part of this book may be
reproduced in any form or by any electronic or mechanical
means, including information storage and retrieval systems,
without permission in writing from the publisher, except
by a reviewer who may quote brief passages in a review.

FIRST EDITION

*The title page photograph of Joseph Shabalala is used by the kind
permission of Michael Brosilow.*

Library of Congress Cataloging-in-Publication Data

Yourgrau, Tug.
    The Song of Jacob Zulu / Tug Yourgrau. — 1st ed.
        p.   cm
    A play inspired by the true story of Andrew Zondo.
    ISBN 1-55970-237-0 (hc)
    ISBN 1-55970-238-9 (pbk)
    1. Trials (Terrorism) — South Africa — Drama.
    2. Executions and executioners — South Africa —
Drama.   3. Zulu (African people) — Drama.   4. Blacks —
South Africa — Drama.   I. Title.
PR9369.3.Y68S65   1993
822 — dc20   93-2327

Published in the United States by Arcade Publishing, Inc.,
New York
Distributed by Little, Brown and Company

HC: 10   9   8   7   6   5   4   3   2   1
PB: 10   9   8   7   6   5   4   3   2   1

BP

PRINTED IN THE UNITED STATES OF AMERICA

To my children, Sarah and David, who are the future,
and to Beth, my wife—
and to the memory of Headman Shabalala

*"He is despised and rejected of men; a man of sorrows, and
acquainted with grief: and we hid as it were our faces from
him: he was despised, and we esteemed him not. Surely he
hath borne our griefs, and carried our sorrows: yet we did
esteem him stricken, smitten of God, and afflicted. But he
was wounded for our transgressions, he was bruised for our
iniquities: the chastisement of our peace was upon him; and
with his stripes we are healed."*

ISAIAH 53: 3–5

Introduction

In the spring of 1987, I returned to South Africa for the first time in nearly thirty years. It was only a ten-day trip — back home, my wife was very pregnant with our twins — but a very evocative and moving time for me nonetheless. I had left the country as a child in 1959. My father, a refugee from Hitler's Germany, wanted to pursue his career as a physicist and philosopher in America. My South African–born mother, a gifted violinist, had run a jazz band as a young woman and had soloed with orchestras in Palestine. Both my parents opposed apartheid but were not activists.

It was during this short trip that I learned about the trial and conviction of a young black South African for committing a gruesome act of terrorism. He had set off a bomb in a crowded shopping center just before Christmas, 1985. When he was hung a few months later, he was barely twenty. What was striking about the young man was that he'd apparently grown up as a devout Christian, a gentle minister's son who eschewed not only violence but politics as well. An excellent student, he had before him opportunities open to only a tiny fraction of his generation. His name was Andrew Zondo. How had he become a murderer?

Two years later, while working as a filmmaker at Boston's WGBH, I obtained copies of South African newspaper stories about the explosion and trial. Carmel Rickard, an able South African journalist who had covered the trial, provided me with background research. I also conducted interviews with American experts on South African law, as well as American and South African journalists and lawyers. Professor

Fatima Meer of the University of Natal, who had been a witness at the trial, provided a large part of the public record transcript to me, which I completed from another source. Her book on the trial was inspiring. Through my research, there emerged the outline of a story of great power, a tragedy like that of the Bible or the Greeks. It was the story of an innocent, bright boy whom the fates — in this case, the apartheid system — ground up and destroyed. It was his special gifts of mind and personality that contributed to his disastrous end. Peter McGhee, now vice president for national programming at WGBH, commissioned me to boil down the public record transcript of the trial into a two-hour teleplay. The completed docudrama did not attract a producer.

From the beginning, however, I was drawn to another treatment of the material, one that also ventured outside the courtroom. Andrew Zondo was from Natal, the same part of South Africa in which I had grown up and from which the magnificent musical group Ladysmith Black Mambazo hail. I had cried the first time I heard Mambazo singing on Paul Simon's *Graceland* album. Their music echoed the gorgeous sounds I had heard as a child on the radio on Sunday mornings. The African people who worked in our home taught my brothers and me African songs that I still remember. Andrew grew up with this music; and in prison, during those days before he died, his fellow inmates must have raised him up to heaven on the wings of these songs.

I decided to tell the story of a young man such as Andrew in the form of a Greek drama, but with an African twist: Aeschylus set in Zululand. The chorus would sing traditional South African songs and would play many roles: first, that of the young man's church congregation; then his high-school mates; next, the

ANC guerrillas with whom he trains; and finally, the audience in the courtroom at his trial. The songs would comment on the protagonist and the action.

I decided to fictionalize the story, to have the central figure stand for the whole generation of young black South Africans who have been sacrificed to history, who are unschooled and potentially explosive. They are victims who, in the tragic cycle of violence in South Africa, claim other innocents as their victims. I was drawn also to the complexity of story. How should we see the Zondos of this world: as martyrs crucified on the cross of apartheid (the point of view of one part of the antiapartheid movement) or as primary agents of their own actions and fate? There is no simple answer. A tenet of social psychology, which I believe South Africa bears out, is that inhuman situations brutalize people and make even the best of us capable of inhuman actions. In the Zondo case, racism made a murderer of a devout Christian. But does that mean we should remove all notions of individual moral responsibility?

History, it seems, is a blunt instrument, incapable of making distinctions as fine as those involving a single human life. The great forces of history, such as apartheid and the antiapartheid movement, shift and grind against each other like massive tectonic plates along a fault line, crushing individual people.

In June of 1990, I submitted a short description of my idea to the New Plays Project of the Steppenwolf Theatre Company. A few months later, I also contacted Ladysmith Black Mambazo's business manager and arranged to meet the group on their next U.S. tour. So it was that on a chilly March morning in 1991 I found myself at the coffee shop of the Holiday Inn in Somerville, Massachusetts, a blue-collar town north of Boston, waiting to see Joseph Shabalala, the founder and leader of the group. I encountered a small, brown-skinned man with a big smile and a gentle voice, swaddled in a large parka. He ordered tea with lemon, and we sat down to talk. Joseph liked the idea of the play, its antiviolent theme, very much. We sang the hymn "Jesus Loves Me" together in Zulu: **"Wangithand uJesu lo . . ."** (I'm a Jew, but I'd learned the song as a child.) Joseph harmonized. I was thrilled. Then Joseph came upon Andrew Zondo's name in my notes. He blurted out that this boy was his cousin! He and his group knew the father and had sung in the family church. Both of us were astonished. I heard in my head the sound of the planets realigning themselves. "We must do this," said Joseph. "He is my cousin."

Randall Arney, the artistic director of Steppenwolf, had contacted me in January, nearly nine months (the gestation of a human life) after I had submitted my idea, to tell me I was a finalist. Later, I told him about my wonderful meeting with Mambazo, and in April, after I submitted sample scenes, the company commissioned a play from me. The play was written over the course of the next year, most feverishly in the rehearsals that led to the Steppenwolf opening in the spring of 1992. I kept some of the original language of the trial and I drew on portions of other South African trials. All the characters are composites, especially that of the defense counsel, Marty Frankel, whom I fashioned in part from my own cousins who were lawyers in South Africa and in part from distinguished South African civil rights lawyers, several of whom had been students of my father back in South Africa. I went back to the great Greek dramas, especially Aeschylus's *Orestia* and Sophocles' Oedipus cycle, for inspiration and guidance. I read Genesis, in particular the saga of Jacob, very closely.

I benefited enormously in the writing of this play from the talents of my collaborators. Joseph Shabalala, who created the music and wrote a number of lyrics, is a remarkable musician, a man for whom the label "genuis" is not inappropriate. The music of Mambazo elicits praises of almost embarrassing effusiveness from those who hear it. Theirs is truly the sound of angels come to ground. It is an aural embrace, the voice of community, of uplift, of transcendence. Working with Joseph and "the guys," I was able to reenter, as it were, the world of my childhood and, in a vital way, to make it right and whole. That is a rare privilege and a joy.

A tragedy struck us just before Christmas of 1991. Headman Shabalala, one of the founding members of Ladysmith Black Mambazo, was murdered by an off-duty white security guard back in South Africa. The judge ruled that the killing was "culpable homicide," and he gave the killer a three-year sentence, not necessarily to be served in jail. Headman left behind a widow and several children. It is a testament to the profound courage of Joseph Shabalala and his colleagues that they decided to continue work on the play.

The play would not be what it is without the work of the director, Eric Simonson. The stage pictures he created, especially the opening image of the chorus dancing toward the audience, were extraordinary. But Eric was also an inspired and ruthless editor who forced me to strip the story to its fundamentals and to put each line of dialogue to the acid test. He suggested to me that I introduce a character modeled after the blind prophet Tiresias in *Oedipus Rex*, and this eventually became Itshe.

Improvisations by the actors, in workshops and later in the rehearsals, played a very important part in fleshing out the play. I am indebted to all the actors, but I especially want to single out the magnificent work of Zakes Mokae, who created three roles,

K. Todd Freeman, Pat Bowie, Danny Johnson, and Erika Heard, as well as the three members of the Steppenwolf Acting Ensemble who played in the show: Robert Breuler, John Mahoney, and Alan Wilder.

As I write this, news reports announce the setting of a date in early 1994 for free, democratic elections in South Africa. I wish deeply that this come to pass — and with a minimal loss of life. Nine thousand people have died in political fighting in the three years since Nelson Mandela was freed. A new day may be dawning in South Africa, but the birth is traumatic, and it is still very possible that the labor pangs will kill the child. History, I am afraid, will claim many more victims before a free South Africa comes into being.

It is for these victims, of all races, that *The Song of Jacob Zulu* is sung.

TUG YOURGRAU
June 1993

The Song of Jacob Zulu was developed as part of the New Plays Project of the Steppenwolf Theatre Company, Randall Arney, Artistic Director, Stephen B. Eich, Managing Director. The project was made possible through the generous funding of the Joyce Foundation.

The Song of Jacob Zulu opened on April 12, 1992, at the Steppenwolf Theatre in Chicago with the following cast:

MRS. ZULU, MRS. NGOBESE, MA BUTHELEZI	Pat Bowie
JUDGE NEVILLE	Robert Breuler
MAGISTRATE, MR. JEPPE	Patrick Clear
JOHN DAWKINS, DR. SHAW	David Connelly
MARTIN ZULU, ZEBULUN, GUERRILLA	Leelai Demoz
MRS. VAN HEERDEN	Deanna Dunagan
JACOB ZULU	K. Todd Freeman
MRS. SABELO, BEAUTY DLAMINI, GUERRILLA	Erika L. Heard
INTERPRETER, FUMANI, GUERRILLA, JACOB'S SUPERIOR	Danny Johnson
MARTY FRANKEL	John Mahoney
POLICEMAN, MBONGENI, MICHAEL DUBE, GUERRILLA, PHILIP ZULU	Gary DeWitt Marshall
REV. ZULU, MR. X, ITSHE	Zakes Mokae
AUNT MIRIAM, STUDENT, RUTH DUBE	Tania Richard
ANTHONY DENT, LIEUTENANT MALAN	Alan Wilder
MICHAEL JEPPE, LIEUTENANT KRAMER	Nicholas Cross Wodtke
MR. VILAKAZI, UNCLE MDISHWA, TEACHER, POLICEMAN, PERCY, COMMISSAR	Cedric Young
CHORUS LEADER	Joseph Shabalala

CHORUS   *Ladysmith Black Mambazo:* Jabulani Dubazana, Abednego Mazibuko, Albert Mazibuko, Geophrey Mdletshe, Russel Mthembu, Inos Phungula, Jockey Shabalala, Ben Shabalala, Joseph Shabalala.

From May 19-24, 1992, Tania Richard played MRS. VAN HEERDEN.

DIRECTOR: ERIC SIMONSON

Original Music composed by Ladysmith Black Mambazo
Lyrics: Tug Yourgrau and Ladysmith Black Mambazo

Set Design: Kevin Rigdon
Costume Design: Erin Quigley
Lighting Design: Robert Christen
Sound Design: Rob Milburn
Production Stage Manager: Malcolm Ewen
Stage Manager: Alden Vasquez
Dialect Coach: Gillian Lane-Plescia
Fight Director: Ned Mochel

The Song of Jacob Zulu opened on January 30, 1993, at the Steppenwolf Theatre in Chicago; on February 23, 1993, at His Majesty's Theatre, Perth, Australia, as part of the Festival of Perth, David Blekinsop, Director; and on March 24, 1993, at The Plymouth Theatre in New York, the Steppenwolf Theatre, Randall Arney, Stephen Eich, Albert Poland, Susan Liederman and Bette Cerf Hill, Producers, in association with Maurice Rosenfield, with the following cast:

MARTY FRANKEL	Gerry Becker
MRS. ZULU, MRS. NGOBESE, MA BUTHELEZI	Pat Bowie
JUDGE NEVILLE	Robert Breuler
JOHN DAWKINS, DR. SHAW	David Connelly
MARTIN ZULU, ZEBULUN, GUERRILLA	Leelai Demoz
JACOB ZULU	K. Todd Freeman
MRS. SABELO, BEAUTY DLAMINI, GUERRILLA	Erika L. Heard
MR. VILAKAZI, FUMANI, GUERRILLA	Danny Johnson
POLICEMAN, MBONGENI, MICHAEL DUBE, GUERRILLA, PHILIP ZULU	Gary DeWitt Marshall
REV. ZULU, MR. X, ITSHE	Zakes Mokae
MAGISTRATE, MR. VAN HEERDEN, MR. JEPPE	Don Oreskes
AUNT MIRIAM, STUDENT, RUTH DUBE	Tania Richard
INTERPRETER, POLICEMAN, STUDENT, JACOB'S SUPERIOR	Seth Sibanda
ANTHONY DENT, LIEUTENANT MALAN	Alan Wilder
MICHAEL JEPPE, LIEUTENANT KRAMER	Nicholas Cross Wodtke
POLICEMAN, UNCLE MDISHWA, TEACHER, PERCY, COMMISSAR	Cedric Young
CHORUS LEADER	Joseph Shabalala

CHORUS   *Ladysmith Black Mambazo:* Jabulani Dubazana, Abednego Mazibuko, Albert Mazibuko, Geophrey Mdletshe, Russel Mthembu, Inos Phungula, Jockey Shabalala, Ben Shabalala, Joseph Shabalala.

DIRECTOR: ERIC SIMONSON

Original Music composed by Ladysmith Black Mambazo
Lyrics: Tug Yourgrau and Ladysmith Black Mambazo
Set Design: Kevin Rigdon

Costume Design: Erin Quigley
Lighting Design: Robert Christen
Sound Design: Rob Milburn
Production Stage Manager: Malcolm Ewen
Stage Manager: Alden Vasquez
Dialect Coach: Gillian Lane-Plescia
Fight Director: Ned Mochel

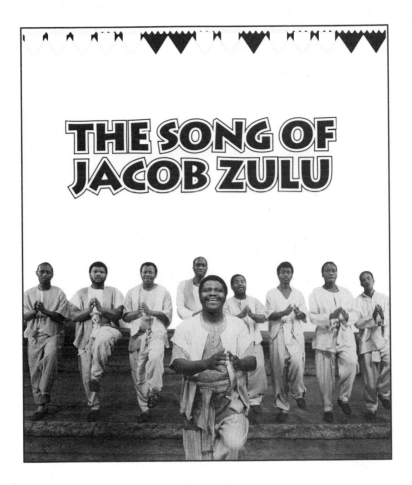

Characters

CHORUS
CHORUS LEADER
SHOPPERS and WORKERS
   at the Shaka's Rock Mall
MAGISTRATE
INTERPRETER
PRISON GUARDS
JACOB ZULU
MRS. SIBONGILE ZULU
REV. HEZEKAYA ZULU
MARTY FRANKEL
GUARD
MARTIN ZULU
BEAUTY DLAMINI
CONGREGATION
UNCLE MDISHWA
AUNT MIRIAM
JUDGE HARRY NEVILLE
ANTHONY DENT
MRS. IDA NGOBESE
PAULUS VAN HEERDEN
JOHN DAWKINS

MRS. VICTORIA SABELO
THOMPSON VILAKAZI
MICHAEL JEPPE
MR. JEPPE
MR. X (DONALD THWALA)
DR. JONATHAN SHAW
FUMANI
STUDENTS
TEACHER
LIEUTENANT KRAMER
LIEUTENANT MALAN
ZEBULUN
MBONGENI
PERCY
MA BUTHELEZI
ITSHE
RUTH DUBE
MICHAEL DUBE
GUERRILLAS
COMMISSAR
JACOB'S SUPERIOR
PHILIP ZULU

The actors are meant to play several roles. The actor playing JACOB ZULU should play only that role.

The Setting

The play is fictional. The characters and events are composites, drawn from the history of South Africa over the last twenty-five years.

The main action takes place in a fictional courtroom, the Supreme Court of South Africa, Pietermaritzburg Division, located in the small inland town of Eshowe in the province of Natal, the principal Zulu-speaking region of the country. Upstage center stands a chair representing the judicial bench where sits the JUDGE. *Just above and behind the* JUDGE *is the coat of arms of South Africa, a rampant oryx and a springbok framing a shield. Upstage right is the witness box; upstage left is the dock to which* JACOB ZULU *is brought.* JACOB *faces down onto the audience, which is in the position of spectators at the trial.* MARTY FRANKEL, *the defense attorney, stands or sits to one side of the stage, and* ANTHONY DENT, *the prosecutor, stands or sits on the other side.*

The open area downstage center will be the principal arena to reenact flashbacks, such as JACOB's *baptism in* REV. ZULU's *church or the police attack on* JACOB's *school. The different settings should be suggested minimally, principally by changes in lighting. The staging must shift swiftly between past and present.*

The CHORUS *should be integrated into the staging of the play as much as possible.*

Act
O N E

Scene 1

Black. The song begins.

(Offstage)

LEADER **Lalelani! [Listen!]**

CHORUS **Lalelani, lalelani!**

   (Repeat between verses.)

(The lights come up half-full. The LEADER AND CHORUS enter. Slowly the lights come up full. The singing grows louder.)

LEADER **The fire is burning**
   It lights up the sky
   From high on the rock
   Down to the sea.
   It is taking the children.
   It is eating the future.

   Smother the fire, open your hearts.

   (Repeat three times.)

CHORUS **Smother the fire, open your hearts.**

   (Repeat twice.)

LEADER **This is the song of a young man called**
   Jacob Zulu . . .

CHORUS **Zulu!**

LEADER **Who suffered for the sins of South**
   Africa . . .

CHORUS **South Africa!**

LEADER **This is a song of those for whom the good**
   news . . .

5

CHORUS **The good news, the good news, the good news!**

LEADER **Of the end of apartheid . . .**

CHORUS **If it really is the end . . .**
Amen.

LEADER **Comes too late.**

CHORUS **Amen. Hallelujah!**
Lalelani, lalelani . . .

(Repeat last line until explosion.)

(The lights change. Tinny Christmas carols play offstage. It is now the morning of December 24, 1985, at the Shaka's Rock Shopping Mall. SHOPPERS and WORKERS enter and go through the motions of a day at the mall. After several seconds, there is a shocking flash of light and a loud explosion. The SHOPPERS and WORKERS twist and slump to the floor in slow motion, miming terrible injuries. Screams and sirens erupt, but in stylized, hyper-real fashion, to match the slow motion of the falling bodies. A montage of radio reports follows immediately. The ANNOUNCERS' voices overlap and intertwine.)

FEMALE RADIO ANNOUNCER *(Over loudspeaker)* This is a bulletin from the Metropolitan News Service. A bomb has just exploded at a crowded shopping center in the coastal resort town of Shaka's Rock in Natal. At least four people are believed dead and fifty injured in what authorities are calling the worst-ever incidence of political violence in the Durban area. . . .

MALE AFRIKAANS RADIO ANNOUNCER *(Over loudspeaker)* **Hier volg n nuusberig van die SAUK. n Bom het omstreeks tienuur vanoggend in die winkelscompleks by Shaka's Rock in Natal ontplof en vier mense is alreeds dood . . .** [This is a news bulletin from the SABC. A bomb exploded around ten o'clock this morning in a shopping center at Shaka's Rock in Natal, and four people are already dead.]

6

MALE RADIO ANNOUNCER We interrupt our regular programming to bring you this news update.

MALE ZULU RADIO ANNOUNCER *(Over loudspeaker)* **Zona umsakazo wesizulu nanku umbiko ophuthumayo kuphume ibhomu e Shaka's Rock e Natal. Kwafa abantu abane ukuqhuma kwenzeke nge hora leshumi ekuseni. Amaphoyisa asola i ANC ukuthi iyona eyenze lokhu.** . . . [We interrupt our regular program to bring you this news flash. At least four people may have died in a bomb blast in Shaka's Rock in Natal. The bombing took place around ten this morning. Police suspect it is the work of the banned African National Congress.]

FEMALE RADIO ANNOUNCER #2 *(Over loudspeaker)* Emergency crews and ambulances are still clearing the injured. Colonel Johannes Kleynhans of the Natal SAP said that a massive manhunt has been launched for those responsible and warned the public that the outlawed African National Congress . . .

(Before the radio montage fades out, the CHORUS *cross through the fallen bodies. As the* CHORUS *pass them, the* VICTIMS *get up slowly and exit.)*

CHORUS **Lalelani, lalelani!**

(Repeat between verses.)

LEADER **It is taking the children.
It is eating the future.**

(The MAGISTRATE, *a middle-aged white man, and the black* INTERPRETER *enter with a table and chair, which they set up downstage. Two* BLACK PRISON GUARDS *also enter, hauling* JACOB ZULU *before the* MAGISTRATE. JACOB *is a nineteen-year-old black South African, his face puffy and bruised. He is wearing a gray prison jumpsuit, and his wrists are shackled. The lights change.)*

Scene 2

Interrogation Room at a jail in Pietermaritzburg. It is December 29, 1985.

MAGISTRATE Tell the prisoner he may make his statement.

INTERPRETER **Yenzake isitatiminde sakho.**

(JACOB *limps downstage and delivers his statement to the audience.*)

JACOB **Ngifuna ukunitshela ukuthi umuntu obeke ibomb e Shaka's Rock yimi. Ngilibeke ibomb ngo ten thirty ekuseni. Ngilibeke ibomb ngicabanga ukuthi lizoqhuna emanithini angu twenty homa thirty enva kokulifaka emgqonyeni ka doti phambi kwehovisi le South African Airways. Injongo yami bengifuna ukuqhumisa ihovisi hayi ukubulala abantu lapho. Yilokho engifuna ukukusho lapha phambi kwe Mantshi.**

INTERPRETER *(Simultaneous translation)* I want to say that the man who planted the bomb at Shaka's Rock is myself. I planted the bomb at 10:30 A.M. in a refuse bin in front of the offices of the South African Airways.

JACOB I expected it to explode twenty to thirty minutes later. My intention was to blow up those offices, not to kill people who might be there. I committed the offense by myself. No one else was with me.

LEADER **So . . .**

(*The* LEADER *circles around* JACOB.)

CHORUS **You are the one,
You are the one,
Who committed this murder,**

> This horror,
> This tragedy,
> This shame?!

LEADER   **Is your heart like a stone? Who are you?**

CHORUS   **Who are you?**

LEADER   **Why, Jacob, why?**

CHORUS   **Why, why, why, why, why?**
   (Repeat three times.)

MAGISTRATE   **Ja,** the prisoner claims that the arresting officers beat him. Tell him to show me the bruises.

INTERPRETER   **Uma kukhona lapho ulimele khona, amanxeba nemivimbi, kuveze manje.** [He says that if you have any injuries or bruises or abrasions, you must show them to him now.]

(As JACOB *speaks, the* GUARDS *roughly examine the injuries he describes on his face and body. One* GUARD *makes notes. The* CHORUS *mutter expressions of sympathy as* JACOB's *wounds are shown.)*

JACOB   **Bangishaye emlonyeni, emahlombe, ezingal-weni, nasokhalweni, bangishaye ngento la.** *(He points to his hip.)*

INTERPRETER   *(Simultaneously)* I have a cut on the upper lip. On my right shoulder I have abrasion marks. On my left upper arm I show a small puncture wound and here on my hip.

JACOB   My top front teeth are loose where they hit me. They punched me here *(pointing to his left cheek)* and here *(pointing to his right ear).* They cut me on my belly. The police hit me all over. *(Beat)* I'm just telling you what happened. You can do with it what you like. I don't expect to get any special treatment.

(The Guards, Magistrate *and* Interpreter *exit.* Jacob *crosses downstage and sits down. The* Chorus *cross toward* Jacob.)

Leader　**So, they beat you!**

Chorus　**Mmm, poor boy!**

Leader　**Did they beat these words from you?**

Chorus　**Mmm, poor boy!**

Leader　**In white South Africa,
They hate you.**

Chorus　**Bayakuzonda, mfana, bayakuzonda!**
[They hate you, boy, they hate you!]

(Repeat the last line three times.)

(The Chorus *lift* Jacob *up and cross with him to stage left. Simultaneously,* Mrs. Zulu, Jacob's *mother, a tired-looking woman in her mid-forties, enters, as does a* Black Prison Guard, *who sets up a chair upstage left. The* Chorus *seat* Jacob *on the chair and dance off upstage.)*

Scene 3

Visitors room, Eshowe Courthouse Jail, Thursday, February 6, 1986. Mrs. Zulu *kneels next to* Jacob, *who stares ahead impassively.* Rev. Hezekaya Zulu, *a middle-aged black minister wearing an old, dark suit, enters stage right with* Marty Frankel, *a middle-aged Jewish lawyer. They cross to* Jacob.

Rev. Zulu　Do you think you can help us, **Mnumzana** [Sir]?

Frankel　I really don't know, **Umfundisi** [Reverend]. I just took the case this morning. *(Beat, checking his watch.)* All right, we haven't much time. *(Beat)* OK, when the judge asks you how do you plead, you are to say, "Not guilty."

Rev. Zulu　*(To* Jacob*)* Not guilty, not guilty.

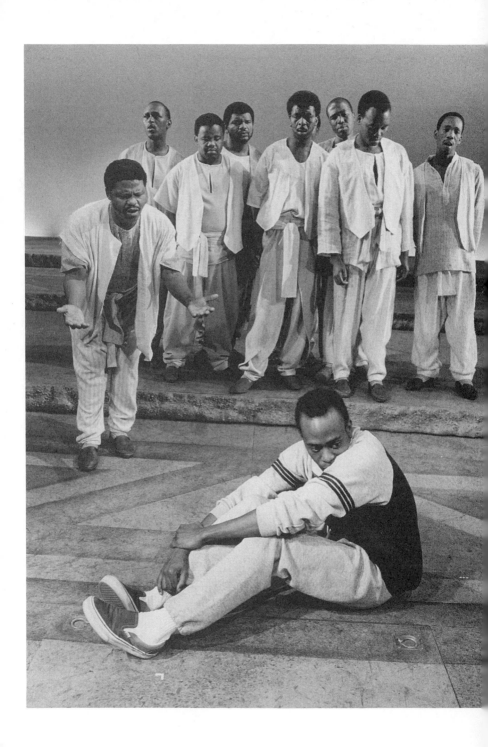

FRANKEL   Do you understand? (JACOB *doesn't respond.*)
He understands?

REV. ZULU   Yes, sir.

FRANKEL   You've got to plead *not guilty.*
(JACOB *sits impassively.*)

MRS. ZULU   Please. Please. Do as he says.

FRANKEL   I mean, I have to be blunt, **Umfundisi.**
There's very little chance of your son coming out
of this alive. Very little. Not after his confession.
But there is *no* chance at all if he won't plead not
guilty.
(A GUARD *enters.*)

GUARD   Three minutes.

REV. ZULU   What?
(*The* GUARD *exits.*)

CHORUS   **Cabanga, imagine!**
           (*Repeat under dialogue.*)

MRS. ZULU   Jacob! Jacob!

FRANKEL   I need to look over the evidence. But he's
simply got to tell me more. I cannot construct a
defense on the basis of what he's told me so far.

MRS. ZULU   You've got to cooperate with him.

FRANKEL   You saw what it's like out there. It's an
armed camp. Every newspaper and TV in the
country. They're all howling for blood.

MRS. ZULU   My God, my God! I can't imagine him
hurting anyone.

REV. ZULU   Look, you don't know my son. He's not a
criminal.
(FRANKEL *nods.*)

Mrs. Zulu   He came to Christ just four years ago.

Rev. Zulu   I baptized him myself, I remember the day exactly. Imagine, **cabanga!**

(Rev. and Mrs. Zulu cross downstage center with Jacob. The lights change. We are now in Rev. Zulu's impoverished church in Imbali Township outside Pietermaritzburg. It is June 1982. There is a simple baptism font downstage center. The Chorus are now the Choir. Martin, Jacob's ten-year-old brother, and Beauty Dlamini, a fifteen-year-old black girl, enter with other Members of the Congregation. Rev. Zulu dons his vestment, Jacob puts on a white robe.)

Chorus   **Cabanga! Imagine, imagine, imagine.**

(Continue under Leader.)

Leader   **Can you imagine
How it must be
For the parents?
They have not seen the boy
For two years!
The boy they remember
Is a boy who heard the good news.**

Chorus   **The good news, the good news, the good news!**

(Beat)
**uJesu wayibekingoma,
Emlonyeni wami
Ukuze ngidumise igama lakhe**

**Emakholweni
Ahlanziweyo ngegazi**

**Ewe ewe Nkosi yami   .
Umphefumlo wami
Wophumula kuwe.**

[Jesus put the music in my mouth
So that I may praise His name.

Jesus fills His children with music
So that they may be saved.

12

    Yes, yes, my Lord.
    My soul will rest with You.]

(JACOB *is transformed. He has a shy intensity, a charisma that draws people to him.*)

REV. ZULU What a day, what a time, what a day, what a time! Brothers and Sisters, today Jacob's sins will be washed away in the blood of the Lamb!

CONGREGATION Hallelujah!

REV. ZULU Today the Holy Spirit will fill his heart and cleanse his soul!

CONGREGATION Hallelujah!

REV. ZULU Today, **Nkosi** [Lord], we are also mindful of our oldest son, Philip, whom You have taken to sit on Your right-hand side.

CONGREGATION Amen.

(REV. ZULU *steps into the font, followed by* CHORUS MEMBERS, *who help* JACOB *into the font.*)

REV. ZULU Jacob, Jacob, Jacob, do you accept into your heart Christ Jesus as your Savior?

JACOB **Yebo [Yes], Baba, yebo.**

REV. ZULU Will you walk in His path, the path of peace, the path of righteousness everlasting?

JACOB **Yebo, Baba, yebo, kunjalo**.

(REV. ZULU *pours water on* JACOB's *bowed head.*)

REV. ZULU I baptize you in the name of the Father, of the Son, and of the Holy Ghost. *(Chanting)* We-are-buried-with-Christ-in-baptism-in-the-likeness-of-His-death-and-raised-up-reborn-to-eternal-life! **uMoya oyiNgewele!** [Holy Spirit!]

(*The* CONGREGATION *explode with shouts of* "Hallelujah!" *and* "Amen!" REV. ZULU, MRS. ZULU *and the* CHORUS *hug the dripping, shivering boy.* JACOB *is exultant. He reaches for* MARTIN *and hugs him.*)

CONGREGATION **My, my, my,
Jesus is my,
My, my, my,
Jesus is my,
Jesus is my Savior
Day by day
My, my, my.**

*(*UNCLE MDISHWA *and* AUNT MIRIAM *enter. The* UNCLE *is drunk, and he brandishes a large goatskin.)*

UNCLE MDISHWA *(Shouting)* Happy days! Happy days!

AUNT MIRIAM **Halala,** Jacob, **halala!** [Congratulations!]

*(*UNCLE MDISHWA *places the goatskin around* JACOB*'s shoulders.)*

UNCLE MDISHWA We brought the **iskhumba sembuzi** [goatskin].

REV. ZULU **Haikona!** [No!] No, no! Take that thing off him!

AUNT MIRIAM Hezekaya! What has got into you? We all put on the goatskin. You put it on.

REV. ZULU That was before I heard the Word of the Lord.

AUNT MIRIAM And now it is Jacob's turn. Do you want the ancestors, the **amaDlozi,** to get angry with the boy?

UNCLE MDISHWA **Yebo,** very angry.

MRS. ZULU *(To* REV. ZULU*)* Let them, dear, let them.

JACOB **Baba,** please.

REV. ZULU No. This is a House of the Lord. There's no place here for this superstition.

UNCLE MDISHWA **Aya, madoda, Uya bheda'lo?!** [Man, what are you talking about?!] What are you calling superstition?

14

(The CONGREGATION *now jump in on different sides. There is much shoving and argument.)*

JACOB   **Baba, Baba,** it's Mama's family. They're just paying their respects. I'm happy to put it on.

REV. ZULU   I said no.

JACOB   **Baba,** please. *(Beat)* Philip wore the goatskin. I know he'd want me to wear it too.

MRS. ZULU   Hezekaya, I understand how you feel. But this is Jacob's day. Let him have his way.

JACOB   Just this one time, **Baba,** please.

REV. ZULU   *(Pause)* Oh, all right.

CONGREGATION   Hallelujah!

AUNT MIRIAM   May our sacrifice, **amaDlozi,** bring peace to your restless souls and make straight and safe the path this beautiful boy will walk. Hallelujah!

CONGREGATION   Amen, hallelujah!

JACOB   *(Starts singing and dancing around in the goatskin.)*

My, my, my,
Jesus is my,
My, my my,
Jesus is my,
Jesus is my Savior
Day by day
My, my, my.

(The CONGREGATION, REV. ZULU *and the* RELATIVES *take up the song. The good mood is restored. The lights fade down on the church. The lights come up full downstage left.* REV. ZULU, MRS. ZULU *and* JACOB *cross back to* MR. FRANKEL. *We are back in the Eshowe Jail visitors room.)*

REV. ZULU   That is our son Jacob.

MRS. ZULU   He's a good boy. Everybody, they all loved him.

REV. ZULU   You must tell him that. The judge.
(The GUARD *enters.)*

GUARD   It is time.

FRANKEL   Now remember. Not guilty.
(They exit.)

Scene 4

The LEADER *enters, wearing a blood-red robe.*

LEADER   **Ayikanoni!** [The time is not right!]
(The CHORUS *enters in two groups, from opposite sides of the stage.)*

CHORUS   **Ayikanoni imbuz'embovu,**
Ayikahlatshwa!
[The time is not right to fight!]
(Repeat twice.)

(The two lines form one line, facing the audience.)

LEADER   **Wobuya sibhamu sami siwile.**
[My gun is falling.]

CHORUS   **Siwile, siwile, siwile.**
[Falling, falling, falling.]

LEADER   **Abhayisikili!** [Amazing!]

CHORUS   **Abhayisikili likhwelwa ngomesisi**
Abafazi babelungu bhayisikili!
[We are seeing amazing things!]
(Repeat twice.)

LEADER   **Ayihlale phansi!** [Sit down!]

CHORUS   **Ayihlale phansi ibamb' umthetho,**
Ayihlale phansi!
[Sit down and keep in order!]
(Repeat twice.)

16

LEADER   **Hlala phansi, sengihleli!** [Sit down!]

CHORUS   **Sengihleli.** [I'm sitting.]
         (Repeat several times.)

LEADER   **Emangweni!**

CHORUS   **Izithulu!** [Peace, my brothers!]
         (Repeat twice.)
         (Beat)

LEADER   **Laqalicala!** [The trial begins!]

CHORUS   **Icala, laqala, icala!** [The trial begins!]

LEADER   **Laqala, madoda!**

CHORUS   **Icala, laqala, icala!**
         (Repeat under the LEADER.*)*

LEADER   **Now begins the trial of Jacob Zulu.**

*(*JUDGE HARRY NEVILLE, *a white man in his sixties, enters and crosses downstage. He is known as a liberal in South African terms. The* LEADER *crosses to him.)*

LEADER   **Here there is no jury, no council of elders.**

(The LEADER *takes off his robe and puts it on the* JUDGE.*)*

LEADER   **Only a judge in a robe of blood.**

(The JUDGE *crosses slowly to the judicial bench and mounts it. The* LEADER *pursues him.)*

LEADER   **What can *he* know of a black man's life?
         Can there be justice?**

CHORUS   **Can there be justice
         For a black man
         In a white man's court
         In South Africa,
         The land of apartheid?**

LEADER   **The land of apartheid!**

(The JUDGE *slams down the gavel several times. The lights change. The* LEADER *and the* CHORUS *cross downstage. We are now in the Eshowe Courtroom.)*

LEADER **Emangweni!**

CHORUS **Izithulu!**

(Repeat several times under.)

(The prosecutor, ANTHONY DENT, a white man in his forties, FRANKEL and the INTERPRETER enter. DENT and FRANKEL wear black judicial robes. A GUARD brings JACOB into the dock.)

JUDGE *(Over the CHORUS's singing)* In the Supreme Court of South Africa, Pietermaritzburg Division, the sixth of February, 1986. The State versus Jacob Themba Zulu, age nineteen, of 46 Dube Road, Imbali. The Accused is charged with the crime of murder in that upon 24 December 1985, at Shaka's Rock Shopping Mall, Shaka's Rock, the Accused killed four persons and attempted to kill other members of the general public. *(Beat)* How do you plead?

INTERPRETER **Uyavuma noma uyaphika na?**

JACOB **Angina cala.**

INTERPRETER He says he pleads not guilty.

JUDGE Very well. *(Beat)* Mr. Dent?

DENT M'Lord, many of the witnesses have traveled some distance to be here, and it is my intention to call as many of them today as possible.

JUDGE I think that's quite right, Mr. Dent, to do so.

DENT The State calls Mrs. Ida Ngobese.

(MRS. NGOBESE, a middle-aged black woman, her left eye covered by a gauze patch, enters and crosses to the witness stand. A spotlight falls on her. The last line of her testimony will overlap the first sentence of the next witness, as will be the case for all the other witnesses, to create a montage.)

DENT Are you employed by Mr. and Mrs. Cohen of Pietermaritzburg?

NGOBESE That is so.

DENT Why were you at the Shaka's Rock Mall on the 24 December 1985?

NGOBESE My lady employer had sent me there to buy Keep Kleen.

JUDGE To buy what?

INTERPRETER / CHORUS Keep Kleen!

DENT Keep Kleen. It's a kind of laundry detergent, M'Lord.

JUDGE Ah, yes, thank you. Please go on.

DENT Did you take two-year-old Samuel and seven-year-old Rachel Cohen with you?

NGOBESE Yes.

DENT What happened to you at the shopping mall?

NGOBESE Something struck me. *(She points at her eye.)*

DENT And what happened to Samuel?

CHORUS *(Chanting under)*
Hallelujah!

NGOBESE Little Sammy grabbed me by the left wrist. Then he let go. Then his eyeballs turned up inside his head. *(She weeps.)* As far as I know, he died right there where we fell. *(Beat)* How could I know the bomb was going to go off there? It's not my fault. I don't want anything to do with this bombing and shooting.

(The spotlight fades on MRS. NGOBESE *and comes up on* PAULUS VAN HEERDEN, *a middle-aged Afrikaans-speaking white man.* VAN HEERDEN *turns slowly, showing his wounds to the* JUDGE.)

VAN HEERDEN **Ek het 'n groot sny agter in my been gekry, wat heeltemal oopgevlek was. Hierdie been was vol gate gewees, en ook op my boude vol gate gewees. Ek het my gehoor in hierdie oor verloor, ja. Ek was drie weke in hospital in Durban. [I had a** large cut on the back of my leg. There were holes all over this leg; the same with my buttocks. I lost my hearing in the one ear, yes. I spent three weeks in the hospital in Durban.]

(The spotlight fades on VAN HEERDEN *and comes up on* JOHN DAWKINS, *a middle-aged white man.)*

DAWKINS My first instinct was to run out of the shop. I didn't know what had happened. Everything was black, these like, flames. *(Beat)* I got a hole in the back and stomach. My wife, she got holes all over her chest. She had to undergo surgery a week later. My son, both his arms were full of shrapnel. My daughter had a . . . I'd say like a chunk taken out of her leg. *(Beat)* She was in hospital for eight days. She still can't walk properly. *(Beat)* You see what these people are? Animals, just animals. He doesn't deserve a trial.

(The spotlight fades on DAWKINS *and comes up on* MRS. VICTORIA SABELO, *a middle-aged black woman.)*

SABELO I was injured on both legs. But the right leg was the most seriously injured one, with all the muscles severed. I nearly lost that leg. *(Beat, to* JACOB*)* **Cishe nganqamuka umlenze angisakwazi ukusabenza, nginezingane ezimblili ngizozondla ngani.** [I've got two children. I can't work now. How am I supposed to feed them?]

(The spotlight dims on SABELO *and comes up on* THOMPSON VILAKAZI, *a black man in his forties.)*

VILAKAZI She was lying opposite me. She sat up and . . . and she called, "**Baba?**" *(Beat)* And then she fell right back. And then they took her out.

*(*VILAKAZI *exits.* MICHAEL JEPPE, *a white man in his early twenties, is pushed to the witness stand in a wheelchair by his father,* MR. JEPPE.)*

JEPPE I shouted at her. She didn't move. She just looked at me and turned away.

DENT Are you able to walk at all?

JEPPE No, I can't.

DENT Now *(beat)* did your sister, Anne, die later on that day?

JEPPE **Ja,** she did.

DENT And apart from the physical effects, what has the mental or emotional effect been on you personally?

JEPPE Well, my nerves are all shattered, because whenever lightning goes or I hear a loud sound, I just break down and cry and my father's got to hold me. *(Clutches at his father.)* I think it's affected my father the most. He just sits in our living room day in and day out talking to photographs. *(He breaks down in tears.)*

MR. JEPPE Can we please stop this? My boy is very upset. Can we please stop?

JEPPE It feels like everything's a big mess. Just a total mess.

(He weeps, clutching his father.)

JUDGE Thank you, Mr. Jeppe. Mr. Frankel?

(MR. JEPPE slowly pushes his son stage left.)

FRANKEL No questions, M'Lord.

DENT The State calls no further victims, M'Lord.

JUDGE Very well, Mr. Dent. Given the lateness of the hour, I think it best to adjourn for the day. Court will reconvene tomorrow morning at —

MR. JEPPE **Jou hond!** [You dog!]

(MR. JEPPE punches JACOB in the face. JACOB scrambles back. Pandemonium erupts. The CHORUS cross upstage, shouting at the GUARDS and MR. JEPPE.)

JUDGE Just a moment. Can you please tell me what happened there? I didn't see. *(Bangs gavel.)* Order, order!

(ALL *exit, except the* CHORUS.)

CHORUS MEMBER #1	**An eye for an eye, a tooth for a tooth!**
CHORUS	**Mmhmm,mmhmm,mmhmm, Mhmm, mhmm.**
LEADER	**In South Africa There has been a curse, A blood-red curse, The curse of revenge, Since white fought black Two hundred years ago At Blood River. From Blood River, Two streams run, One thin white, One thick black. So it has been. Will it still be this way now? Will this be the law of the jungle?**
	Blood River, Encome! [Blood River!]
CHORUS	**Blood River, Blood River.**
LEADER	**Umfula wezinyembezi.** [River of tears.]
CHORUS	**Blood River, Blood River.**
LEADER	**Umfula wegazi.** [River of blood.]
CHORUS	**Tears and blood.**
	(Repeat several times.)

(*The* CHORUS *cross back upstage.*)

Scene 5

The jail visitors room. It is the morning of the second day of the trial. JACOB *and* FRANKEL *are seated in chairs, facing each other.* FRANKEL *is leafing through a file. The* CHORUS *sit on the floor around them.*

FRANKEL We stand a chance with this judge. Neville's not a hanging judge. He'll listen to reason. *(Beat)* Now, your confession. You still stand by it? *(Pause)* All right. You reported various injuries. Your leg, your face. Did they coerce this confession? *(Pause.* JACOB *looks away.)* All right. We'll come back to that. Now, you say you were by yourself, you were alone. *No one* gave you aid or assistance of any kind?

JACOB *(Pause)* What I told was the truth. I was alone. *(He turns in his seat and winces.)*

FRANKEL Are they still beating you?

JACOB It doesn't matter.

FRANKEL I can bring charges against the man who attacked you in court. It might delay things. *(*JACOB *shakes his head.)* All right. *(Beat)* Now . . . why? Why did you place the bomb where you did? *(Beat)* Were you instructed to? *(Pause)* Look, this has got to stop. It's no use clamming up on me. You're obviously **Umkhonto** [Spear]. It was a Soviet-made SPM mini-limpet mine, for Christ sake! You don't just pick those up on the street, you don't learn how to detonate them from the back of a bloody matchbox! So who do you think you're fooling? Me? The prosecutor? *(Pause)* Well, it's your life, my friend, and if you want to give up —

JACOB I'm not your friend.

FRANKEL No, you're not my friend, that's right, but I am your counsel.

JACOB   Well, I did not want you. My father com-
manded me, and so I had to take you.

FRANKEL   Or you wouldn't have counsel.

JACOB   I can defend myself.

FRANKEL   Don't be ridiculous. You've confessed —
confessed — to an *atrocity!* Where was the military
target here? This was a bloody shopping center on
Christmas Eve. Three little children dead. Your own
people, old women, *maimed.* It's out-and-out *terrorism!*
You're the nightmare made flesh, the first wave of the
total onslaught!

JACOB   *(Pause)* I wasn't trying to kill anyone.

FRANKEL   All right, good. *(Beat)* You don't have to convince me. You have to convince the judge.

JACOB   Well, I don't care about the judge. He has no
right to try me.

FRANKEL   No right to try you?

JACOB   No.

FRANKEL   That's irrelevant. You *are* being tried. *(Beat)*
And I'm all you've got, my boy.

JACOB   Great.

FRANKEL   Well, I don't see any ANC lawyers lining up
to take your case. Oh, the ANC must be *furious* with
you. You've made them look like a bunch of
murderers!

JACOB   Well, I don't . . . *(Beat)* You're just part of this
whole racist system.

FRANKEL   Dammit, you listen to me! I was defending
political prisoners when your mama was still wiping
your **umdidi** [rectum]. So don't talk rubbish to me.
(Beat) Look, I chose to take your case. No one . . . *no*

one made me come here. *(Pause)* Please help me to help you. Tell me what happened.

JACOB   *(Pause)* I'm not an informer.

FRANKEL   *(Beat)* You're not an informer.

(FRANKEL *exits. The* CHORUS *cross to* JACOB.)

LEADER   **Oh, Jacob!**

CHORUS   **Oh, Jacob, Jacob, Jacob,**
Is it your pride that pushes away
The hand stretched out to help you?

LEADER   **Oh, Jacob!**

CHORUS   **Oh, Jacob, Jacob, Jacob,**
Listen to him — your mother cries,
Whom can your poor father turn to?

(*The* CHORUS *cross with* JACOB *back to the dock.*)

LEADER   **Nangu egijima.** [Someone is running.]

CHORUS   **Nangu egijima safike samkhathaza.**
[Someone is running — we will wear him down.]
(Repeat twice.)

LEADER   **Ashayusoklazu!** [Join your regiments!]

CHORUS   **Ashayusoklazu!**
(Repeat three times.)

(*The* CHORUS *cross upstage.*)

Scene 6

Lights come up on the courtroom. It is later that same day.

JUDGE   Mr. Dent?

DENT   M'Lord, the witness the State will now call is the Accomplice. (FRANKEL *is shocked.*) This man was with the Accused at the time the offense was committed. We would like to use the customary term Mr. X when referring to this witness.

JUDGE Have you any objection, Mr. Frankel?

FRANKEL Yes. M'Lord, this is the first I have heard of this witness. The State has given the Court no reason why the witness should not testify under his own name.

DENT M'Lord, this man will give evidence that he is a member of a banned terrorist organization, the African National Congress. His life may be in danger if his identity is revealed in court.

JUDGE Yes, very well. Mr. Frankel, under these circumstances, I must yield to the State's request.

DENT Thank you, M'Lord. The State calls Mr. X.

(MR. X, *a middle-aged black man whose real name is* DONALD THWALA, *enters from the rear of the theater. The* CHORUS *cross to him.*)

LEADER **We know who he is.**
What games are they playing?

CHORUS **We know who he is.**

LEADER **In all the black townships.**
We know who he is.

MEMBER #2 **In Imbali . . .**

CHORUS **Imbali.**

MEMBER #2 **In Edendale . . .**

CHORUS **Edendale.**

MEMBER #2 **In Caluza**

CHORUS **Caluza.**

In Gazankulu . . .

26

CHORUS   **Gazankulu.**

LEADER   **We know who he is.**
(The CHORUS *encircle* MR. X.)

CHORUS   **A man who sells his brother
For a handful of silver.**
(Repeat three times.)

MEMBER #3 **Informer!**

CHORUS   **Impimpi!**
(The CHORUS *cross downstage.)*

CHORUS   *(Whispering loudly and gesturing at* MR. X)
It's Donald Thwala!

JUDGE   You may proceed, Mr. Dent.

DENT   Now, Mr. X, could you please tell the
court . . .

LEADER   **Hello, Donald!**

CHORUS   **Hello, Donald!**

DENT   Were you ever recruited to be a member of the
African National Congress?

MR. X   Yes. **Umkhonto we Sizwe.**

JUDGE   The Spear of the . . . what is that?

MR. X   The Spear of the Nation.

DENT   It's the military wing of the ANC, M'Lord.

JUDGE   Yes, of course. Please continue.

DENT   Do you know the Accused before Court?

MR. X   Yes.

DENT   When did you first meet him?

MR. X   It was at the beginning of last December. He
was brought to us by our superior to teach us about
mines and explosives.

(The lights change. Jacob *and* Mr. X *cross downstage. We are in* Jacob's *rented room in Edendale Township. It is December 24, 1985.)*

Mr. X   Geoffrey said you'd been looking for me, man.

Jacob   **Nxa, madoda!** [Damn, man!] Where've you been?

Mr. X   Back home.

Jacob   **Ayi!** Three days I've been trying to find you! Three days! Coming by your house . . . *(Beat)* Didn't you hear what happened?

Mr. X   No, what happened?

Jacob   The **amaBhunu** [Boers], man, the white swine, they bombed Lesotho in their planes! They killed nine of our brothers!

Mr. X   What?

Jacob   *Nine!* And they've ordered me to retaliate. Four days they gave me. That was three days ago. But I could do nothing, *nothing,* because of you! You're the only one who knows where the explosives are, **madoda.** You should have told me where you were going!

Mr. X   I told you, I was back home.

Jacob   Fine! Go get that limpet from where you hid it and come right back here. And don't let anybody see you.

Mr. X   Where are we going?

Jacob   To Shaka's Rock Shopping Mall.

Mr. X   What, *now?*

Jacob   **Yebo,** now.

Mr. X   In daylight?

Jacob   **Yebo!** Go, **madoda,** hurry!

(Mr. X *gets the limpet mine from the* Chorus *downstage. It is in a plastic bag. He hands the bag to* Jacob. Dent *continues questioning, and* Mr. X *answers.*)

Dent   What did you do when you arrived in Shaka's Rock?

Mr. X   We walked to the mall.

(Jacob *and* Mr. X *reenact* Mr. X's *version of planting the bomb.*)

Dent   What then?

Mr. X   We went into a shop. When I came out of the shop, he was standing next to a dustbin. He held the bag in one hand, and with the other hand he took the bomb out of the bag and put it into the bin.

(Jacob *hands the bag back to the* Chorus Member *and crosses slowly back to the dock.*)

Dent   Did you notice if there were many children in the area?

Mr. X   Yes, sir, mostly whites.

Dent   And some black people?

Mr. X   Yes, a few.

Dent   What did you think was going to happen?

Mr. X   I thought that when this bomb exploded, the building would collapse and people would get killed.

(*The* Sound *of an explosion. The flashback ends.* Mr. X *appears back in the witness stand. Lights come back up in the courtroom.*)

Dent   What did you do then?

Mr. X   We took a taxi to the place where he stays, then I walked home.

Dent   Right. Did you see the Accused later on that day?

Mr. X   Yes, sir. At his house. He asked me if I'd heard what happened at Shaka's Rock.

DENT   And his mood appeared to be . . . what?

MR. X   Happy, very happy. He said he'd heard on the radio that four had died at the mall and lots had been hurt. But then he said, "Our brothers in Lesotho were nine, and at Shaka's Rock only four died." He was very unhappy only four died. He wanted to kill more whites.

DENT   Do you know what can happen to people who give evidence against **Umkhonto we Sizwe** or the African National Congress?

MR. X   They say that one who testifies is an informer and a sellout and will be shot.

DENT   But you decided to come forward and give evidence?

MR. X   No, I wanted to tell the truth.

DENT   I have no further questions, M'Lord.

(DENT *crosses to his chair and sits down.*)

JUDGE   Thank you. Mr. Frankel?

(FRANKEL *rises and crosses to the witness stand.*)

FRANKEL   Thank you, M'Lord. Now, Mr. *(Beat)* X. Do you know your age?

MR. X   Forty-five.

FRANKEL   The Accused is *nineteen*.

MR. X   I wouldn't know.

FRANKEL   You're old enough to be his father.

MR. X   Yes.

FRANKEL   So who was leading whom here, Mr. X? Who was leading whom?

MR. X   He was leading me.

FRANKEL So you say. *(Beat)* Now, on the day in question, you claim you were with the Accused. Did he actually say to you that his objective was to kill people at Shaka's Rock Mall?

MR. X When he said this was in retaliation for the brothers who had been killed in Lesotho, then I knew that people were going to be killed.

JUDGE Did the Accused actually say so? Or did you merely infer that?

MR. X He . . . he . . . he did not say that by word of mouth, but such a thought did occur to my mind.

FRANKEL So he never actually *said* his objective was to kill people.

MR. X No.

FRANKEL Now, after the police arrested you, you were scared.

MR. X Yes.

FRANKEL So you decided to cooperate with the police in order to save your own skin.

MR. X No, I wanted to tell the truth.

FRANKEL You wanted to save yourself.

MR. X Only God can save me.

FRANKEL I put it to you, you are *greatly exaggerating* the role of the Accused in order to save yourself. But for the fact that you are in this witness stand today, testifying against the Accused, *you yourself* would be standing in the dock as an Accused.

MR. X *(Pause)* That's not true.

FRANKEL No further questions, M'Lord.

(As MR. X *exits, the* CHORUS *menace him.)*

LEADER   **I smell the stink of fear!**

CHORUS   **What did they do to you?**
Was it the whip, was it the water,
Was it the cudgel, or was it the fist?
Mhmm, mhmm, mhmm.
To get all the words just right.

(Repeat last two lines.)

LEADER   **How did they threaten you?**
Did they say they'd take your life,
Did they say they'd harm your wife?
What did they promise you?
It's all so neat and tidy.
They must have coached you hard . . .

CHORUS   **To get all the words just right!**

(The CHORUS *cross upstage, continuing to hum underneath the rest of the scene.)*

FRANKEL   M'Lord, I would like to now to make an application that the Accused be sent for psychiatric evaluation. M'Lord, I have not been able to get a coherent version of the events from the Accused, and it appears to me that he may be mentally ill. The Accused may not have been responsible for his actions at the time of the alleged offense.

JUDGE   Very well. I will grant Mr. Frankel's application. The State will arrange for the Accused to be examined by a psychiatrist tomorrow morning.

*(*FRANKEL, JACOB *and the* JUDGE *exit.)*

Scene 7

This is a split scene. Upstage, we are in a kraal, a traditional home, in Zululand. The CHORUS *surround one* MEMBER, *who is lying down as if sick. Another* CHORUS MEMBER, *wearing a ritual headdress and waving an oxtail, is an* **Inyanga,** *a diviner, conducting a traditional Zulu healing ceremony. Downstage, we are in a hospital office in Pietermaritzburg.* DR. JONATHAN SHAW, *a white psychiatrist, enters and consults a clipboard he is carrying. It is the morning of Saturday, February 8, 1986.*

CHORUS **Mhmm, mhmm, oh, oh, oh.**
　　　　　(Repeat softly under the scene.)

*(*JACOB *enters.)*

SHAW Hello, Jacob. I'm Dr. Shaw, senior psychiatrist here at the Florence Nightingale. The Court has asked me to examine you. *(Beat)* Do you understand me, or shall I get someone to translate?

JACOB No. English is OK.

SHAW You're sure?

JACOB Yes.

SHAW Well, then, please remove your shoes, shirt and trousers. You can leave on your socks and under-pants. *(Beat)* Go on.

*(*JACOB *undresses. The* LEADER *sings about the healing ceremony and the psychiatric examination.)*

LEADER **Our brother acts so strangely.**
　　　　　How have we offended you, Great Ones,
　　　　　That you would make him sick?

(The LEADER *crosses to* JACOB.*)*

　　　　　Our brother acts so strangely.
　　　　　How have we offended you, Great Ones,
　　　　　That you would make him sick?

SHAW Have you ever had measles?

JACOB Yes.

SHAW Scarlet fever?

JACOB No.

SHAW Asthma or any other kind of respiratory disease?

JACOB   My brother Philip did. His breath stopped.

SHAW   I see. *(Beat)* Do you hear things? Have you been hearing any voices?

JACOB   No.

(SHAW raises his arms and crosses to center stage.)

SHAW   Hold your arms straight out, from your sides. That's right, walk toward me.

(JACOB raises his arms and crosses to SHAW.)

LEADER   **In his kraal we will offer sacrifices to you. Have pity, Forefathers, have pity.**

   (Repeat.)

(SHAW continues to conduct a medical examination. He holds up a finger and moves it back and forth. JACOB follows SHAW's finger with his eyes. SHAW then explores JACOB's abdomen with his hands.)

SHAW   Now, you are aware, aren't you, of the seriousness of your situation?

(The CHORUS stop singing.)

JACOB   Yes.

SHAW   You have been charged with capital offenses? If you are found guilty, you may lose your life?

JACOB   Yes.

SHAW   How do you feel about that?

JACOB   What do you mean?

SHAW   Are you happy or sad or what?

JACOB   Well, I am not happy. I do not want to die.

CHORUS   **Mhmm, mhmm, mhmm.**
   Mhmm, mhmm, mhmm.

   (Repeat for rest of scene.)

(The sick CHORUS MEMBER *shakes violently. He rises and joins the* CHORUS. *The lights change.* JACOB *exits.* DR. SHAW *crosses downstage. The* JUDGE *appears upstage. We are back in the courtroom on Monday morning, February 10, 1986, the third day of the trial.)*

SHAW   I found that everything he said was perfectly relevant and coherent. I might note, M'Lord, that the Accused is an adolescent, and as such he may very well be experiencing something we commonly call "adolescent turmoil." *(Beat)* In conclusion, the Accused is, in my opinion, depressed, but his depression is not due to mental illness and is, quite frankly, perfectly in keeping with the situation in which he finds himself.

JUDGE   Doctor, in your opinion is there any real possibility that the Accused might be suffering from any mental illness or defect?

SHAW   None whatsoever.

JUDGE   Yes. Thank you, Doctor. *(DR. SHAW exits.)* The application to send the Accused for further mental observation is refused.

(The JUDGE *exits. The* CHORUS *cross upstage.)*

Scene 8

The visitors room, Eshowe Courthouse Jail, later that same day. MRS. ZULU, REV. ZULU *and* FRANKEL *are gathered around* JACOB, *who sits in a chair.* JACOB *ignores* FRANKEL. *The* CHORUS *observe the others.*

MRS. ZULU   Let me see your face.

JACOB   I'm all right, Mama. *(Beat)* **Sawubona, Baba.** [Hello, Papa.]

REV. ZULU   Jacob.

FRANKEL   Jacob. *(Beat)* Your parents and I were just talking.

MRS. ZULU   The judge saying you were not sick is very bad.

FRANKEL   It's not only that, but look, this informer. Look. *(Beat)* You told me you were by yourself. I don't know if you're trying to protect this man or what, but his evidence was very damaging. *(Beat)* If you're not going to be honest with me, then there's nothing more I can do for you. Nothing. *(Beat)* Your parents want me to defend you. I want to defend you because I think that it's critical for the future of this country that people in your position be given a fair trial. *(Beat)* But if *you* don't want me, then it's no use. I'll quit.

MRS. ZULU   But we want you to stay.

FRANKEL   But I can't if he won't let me! *(Beat)* I'm sorry, **Nkosikasi** [Ma'am], but I'm up against a stone wall here. *(Beat)* Go ahead and try to defend yourself, if that's what you want. Tell the judge he has no right to try you. You can shout **"Amandla!"** ["Power!"] and wave your fist, and when it's all over, a few weeks from now, I *guarantee it,* you will *hang. (Beat)* Or you can tell me what actually happened, and then I can make the best case for you, and not only for you, but *for whatever organization you think is important.* The judge might just give you a prison sentence. *(Beat)* Jacob, don't you realize? It's not just *this* judge, *this* court. The whole *country's* watching you. You have everyone's attention. What do you want to tell them?

(JACOB stands and walks away from FRANKEL.)

MRS. ZULU   *(Pause)* Hezekaya? Say something!

REV. ZULU   Jacob!

MRS. ZULU   *(To REV. ZULU)* Do something!
(Beat. MRS. ZULU goes up to JACOB.)

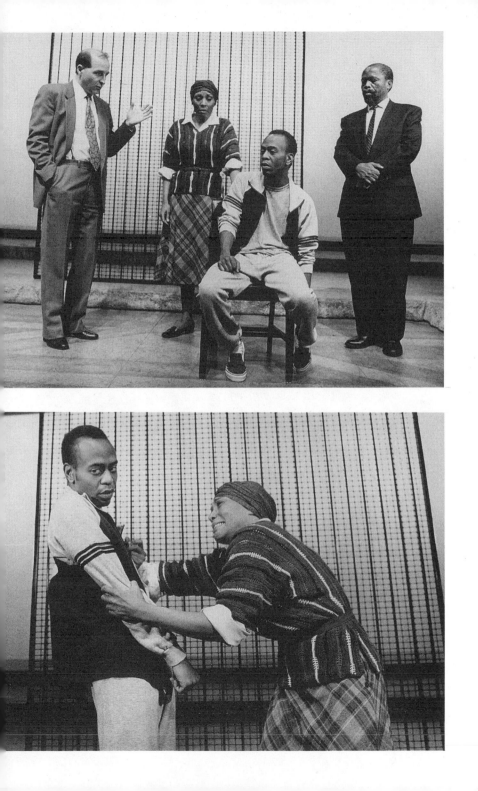

MRS. ZULU Jacob. Jacob. *(Beat)* Look at me.

(JACOB *turns away from* MRS. ZULU. *She struggles to turn him around.)*

JACOB No, no!

MRS. ZULU Look at me, look at me! *(Beat)* You are my child — *my child* — and I will not let you die, I will not let you die, *I will not let you die!*

(They embrace.)

JACOB *(Crying)* I'm so sorry, Mama, I am so sorry.

MRS. ZULU It's all right.

JACOB God will never forgive me. He will never forgive me.

MRS. ZULU It's all right, it's all right. *(Beat)* Let this **Mnumzana** help you. Let him help you.

JACOB *(Pause)* OK, Mama.

FRANKEL Do you really mean that?

JACOB *(Beat)* What do you want to know?

FRANKEL Everything. You say you didn't intend to kill people. Can you prove that?

JACOB *(Beat)* I tried to telephone a warning. To warn the people.

FRANKEL Good.

(MRS. ZULU *embraces* JACOB. *Then she,* REV. ZULU *and* FRANKEL *exit. The* CHORUS *cross to* JACOB.)

LEADER **Ingane yeZulu!** [Child of Heaven!]

CHORUS   **Ingane yeZulu, Child of Heaven,**
          Are you this murderer
          They say you are?
          Let us hear from your mouth
          The kind of man that you are.

LEADER   **It is night, we are lost in the forest.**

The CHORUS *lead* JACOB *back to the dock.*

CHORUS   **Let us hear from your mouth**
          The kind of man that you are.
          It is night, we are lost in the forest.
          Something is out there, we cannot see it.

          (Repeat several times.)

          Let us hear from your mouth
          The kind of man that you are.
          Ingane yeZulu, Child of Heaven!
          Zulu!

(The CHORUS *exit.)*

Scene 9

The courtroom. It is the fourth day of the trial.

JUDGE   Mr. Frankel.

FRANKEL   The Defense calls the Accused, Jacob Zulu.
M'Lord, the Accused is basically Zulu-speaking, but
he chooses to give evidence in English. I have ex-
plained to him that the interpreter will be available.

JUDGE   Both languages are welcome in this court, Mr.
Frankel.

FRANKEL   Now, your father is Reverend Hezekaya
Zulu of the Imbali Evangelical Church?

JACOB   Yes.

FRANKEL And your mother is Mrs. Sibongile Zulu?

JACOB Yes.

FRANKEL Do you have any brothers and sisters?

JACOB No sister. One brother, Martin, who is younger. One older brother, Philip. But he's dead.

FRANKEL Yes. Now, would you tell the Court something of your childhood?

JACOB We were very poor. Even compared to the people around us. *(Beat)* I remember, when we were little, my mother used to go to the mission to get clothes for us. They were all things that white people had worn but did not want anymore. I was ashamed and angry. I thought, What kind of parents do I have who make me wear things which are used and thrown away by other people? Am I some sort of discarded person?

(Offstage, the CHORUS chant under JACOB.)

CHORUS **Umusa kaNkulunkulu!** [Mercy of God!]

JACOB I remember this white minister would come in his car and take us to his home in Pietermaritzburg. His house seemed like a palace to me. Each of his children had their own bedrooms. There was a bathroom right in the house. I was amazed. *(Beat)* His son laughed at me. *(Beat)* I asked myself why my father, who was also a minister, would have so little, and why this white minister and his family would have so much. I don't know. At the time, it was very painful to me. It was like the white minister and his family were living in Heaven and we were living in Hell.

(The chant ends.)

FRANKEL Now, what school did you attend?

JACOB I was in my final year at Imbali High School.

FRANKEL   And were you a good student?

JACOB   Yes, I was.

(MARTIN *enters with a school jacket, which he puts on* JACOB. FUMANI, *a young black man of university age, and two black* HIGH SCHOOL STUDENTS *enter upstage.*)

MARTIN   Come on, Jacob. We'll be late.

FRANKEL   In fact, were you not recommended for a bursary from IBM to study at the University of Pietermaritzburg?

JACOB   Yes, I was.

(JACOB *and* MARTIN *cross upstage. The lights change. We are now on a street near Imbali High School. It is October 1983.* FUMANI *and the* STUDENTS *stop* JACOB *and* MARTIN.)

FUMANI   **Sawubona, umfuwethu!** [Hello, brother!] Are you coming to the meeting after school?

STUDENT #1   Fight this lousy Bantu Education they give us.

STUDENT #2   The **abelungu** [whites], they're just training us to be their slaves, man.

JACOB   **Cha** [no], I'm not going.

STUDENT #1   **Ayi**, don't be like that! Where is your pride, brother?

STUDENT #2   I know this one — he has no pride. He's so full of the white man's religion, he can't see what they're doing to us.

JACOB   I can see, I can see. You don't know what you're talking . . .

(JACOB *and* MARTIN *exit.*)

STUDENT #1   (*Yelling after* JACOB) The revolution begins in your mind, man!

40

STUDENT #2   You think this is the way God wants it to be?

FUMANI   **Wo, abawethu.** [Hold on, guys.] One day he'll come with us. One day he will.

(FUMANI *and* STUDENTS *exit. We are back in the courtroom.*]

FRANKEL   Now, in recent years there have been many protests by black students against the quality of so-called Bantu Education and —

DENT   M'Lord?

JUDGE   Mr. Dent?

DENT   M'Lord, it is open to question why there has been unrest at some black schools in South Africa.

FRANKEL   Well, surely my colleague will agree that the quality of education in black schools is far inferior to that in white schools?

DENT   That is not in the purview of this court to decide, M'Lord.

JUDGE   No, of course not, Mr. Dent. But I will permit Mr. Frankel to finish his question.

(JACOB, HIS CLASSMATES, *including* BEAUTY DLAMINI, *and the* TEACHER, *a weary, officious middle-aged black man, enter.*)

FRANKEL   Thank you, M'Lord. Please tell the Court what happened at your high school in December 1983.

(DENT, FRANKEL *and the* JUDGE *exit. The lights change. We are now in an impoverished Standard Seven classroom at Imbali High School.*)

TEACHER   **Ayi,** what is wrong with you today? Have you all ants in your pants?

(The STUDENTS *sigh and shift in their seats.*)

Can somebody please tell me the names of the prime ministers and presidents of our country? (JACOB's *hand shoots up.*) No, *not* Jacob. We have already heard — too

41

many times — from Master Zulu this morning. There must be *somebody* else, please.

(Pause. JACOB *lifts up* BEAUTY's *hand.)*

TEACHER   Ah, Miss Dlamini to the rescue.

BEAUTY   *(Bored)* Presidents and prime ministers. First there was Louis Botha, then, uh, General Smuts, then . . . let's see . . . Botha, Smuts, then Herzog . . .

(The CHORUS *enter upstage left, dancing the jogging step of the* **toi-toi,** *whistling, shouting, and waving homemade signs that read: BOYCOTT BANTU EDUCATION! LIBERATION BEFORE EDUCATION!)*

LEADER   **Bantu Education!**

CHORUS   **Boycott, boycott!**
         (Repeats five times.)

MEMBER #1   **Uzongena!** [There is someone coming!]

CHORUS   **Umkhonto we Sizwe phuma!**
         [The Spear of the Nation is coming!]
         Shaya amaBhunu, shaya amaBhunu!
         [Strike the Boer!]
         Woza, woza! [Come, come!]
         Umkhonto we Sizwe.
         [Spear of the Nation.]
         Phuma! [Is coming!]

MEMBER #1   **Bantu Education!**

CHORUS   **Boycott! Boycott!**
         (Repeat twice.)

(A few STUDENTS *stand up. The* TEACHER *makes them sit down.)*

TEACHER   Come, come, class! *(To* BEAUTY*)* Go on.

BEAUTY   *(Struggling to speak over the noise)* Then Herzog, then General Smuts again . . .

MEMBER #1　*(Simultaneously)* **Viva, Mandela, viva!**

CHORUS　**Viva!**

MEMBER #1　**Viva, Shaka, viva!**

CHORUS　**Viva!**

MEMBER #1　**Uzongena!**

CHORUS　**Umkhonto we Sizwe phuma.**

LEADER　**Join us! Join us, brothers and sisters!**

(The CHORUS *retreat upstage. Many of the* STUDENTS *try to join the* CHORUS. *The* TEACHER *restrains them.)*

TEACHER　Sit down, sit down!

(The CHORUS *put on police caps and take up truncheons. They now are the* POLICE.*)*

POLICE CAPTAIN　*(Offstage, over a bullhorn)* This is an illegal gathering! I order you to disperse!

(Offstage, SIRENS *start up and grow louder. The* TEACHER *gathers the* STUDENTS *together.)*

TEACHER　**Ayi!** Quickly, quickly.

(The TEACHER *and the* STUDENTS *kneel in a semicircle.)*

TEACHER　Jacob! The Lord's Prayer.

JACOB　**Baba wethu,** who art in heaven, hallowed be Thy Name.

ALL　Thy kingdom come, Thy will be done, on Earth as it is in Heaven. Give us this day our daily bread, and forgive us our trespasses, as we forgive those who trespass against us.

(The CHORUS *jog in step toward the* STUDENTS, *then charge into them, lashing out with truncheons. The lighting and movements become highly stylized.)*

CHORUS　**Shu, shu, shu, shu!** [The sound of tear gas canisters exploding.]

(Screams. The STUDENTS *exit.* JACOB *pushes* BEAUTY *out of danger. The* LEADER *grabs* JACOB *around the throat with his baton and starts to pull him off.* JACOB *wrenches free, but the* LEADER *cracks him across the ear.)*

JACOB   Ah!

*(*JACOB, *clutching his ear, crosses downstage toward the* ZULU *home.)*

LEADER   **Ufile' umuntu,** [Someone's been killed,]

CHORUS   **Ufile' usa dikiza.**
[But the body's still twitching.]

LEADER   **Samthinte sweni,**
[Put your finger in his eye,]

CHORUS   **Impelusadikiza.** [The eye is still twitching.]

(The CHORUS *exit.)*

Scene 10

Afternoon, the same day. The main room of the ZULU *home in Imbali. The only decorations on the walls are old calendars and color pages ripped from magazines.* JACOB *and* REV. ZULU *sit in chairs.* MRS. ZULU *washes* JACOB'S *ear.* MARTIN *looks on.*

REV. ZULU   I don't know what you kids think you're doing.

JACOB   But, **Baba,** how can you say it was *our* fault? Ow! We weren't doing anything.

MRS. ZULU   Put your hand down.

JACOB   But you're hurting me, Mama.

MRS. ZULU   I've got to clean it.

MARTIN   Jacob, did you throw anything at them, huh?

MRS. ZULU   Martin!

REV. ZULU I'm not saying it was your fault.

JACOB I mean, Mr. Mgoduso took us to assembly. We were praying. We were not going —

REV. ZULU I know, I know. You told me already, you *told me!*

MRS. ZULU Hezekaya! Why are you getting angry with the boy?

REV. ZULU Because I want him to listen.

MRS. ZULU Well, he won't if you yell at him.

JACOB **Baba,** it was the kids from Umzinduzi calling us out. We weren't going, we stayed where we were.

MARTIN Jacob, **Baba's** trying to tell you something!

MRS. ZULU Martin, sit down!

REV. ZULU You've . . . you've got to be more *careful.* (*Beat*) When we were your age, they wanted us all to burn our passbooks. Thank goodness your mother and I didn't listen. But your uncle Samuel did. And what happened? Hey? He went to jail! And the police shot some other people. So what good did it do? Nothing! Worse than nothing!! And what about those guys who started the whole thing — where were they? Nowhere — nowhere to be found!

JACOB But, **Baba,** it was the *police,* not us.

REV. ZULU Of course it was the police! How else do you expect the police to act?! (*Beat*) Sibongile, I think we'd better send these kids away somewhere until this is over.

JACOB **Baba,** it's never going to be over. It will —

(REV. ZULU *jumps to his feet.*)

REV. ZULU (*Furious*) Who do you think you are talking to? (*Beat*) You have a bright future ahead of you. I don't want to see you with those kids again. Ever. Do you understand that?

JACOB **Yebo, Baba.**

REV. ZULU Martin?

MARTIN **Yebo.**

(REV. ZULU exits. MRS. ZULU looks at JACOB for a few seconds, then folds JACOB's coat.)

MRS. ZULU Martin.

(MRS. ZULU and MARTIN exit.)

JACOB *(To the audience)* It was from that day onward, whenever I see a policeman I see him as an enemy to me.

(The lights change.)

Scene 11

FUMANI *and a* STUDENT *enter upstage.* JACOB *crosses toward them. It is one week later, on a street near Imbali High School.*

STUDENT There will be seven of us.

FUMANI OK. Be ready at six-thirty. We will pick you up first this time, then go —

JACOB **Sawubona!**

(FUMANI and the STUDENT eye JACOB with suspicion.)

FUMANI *(Pause)* **Sawubona. Kunjani?** [Hello. How are you?]

JACOB Can I talk to you?

(FUMANI gestures for the STUDENT to exit. He does.)

FUMANI OK. What about?

JACOB   The Imbali African Students Organization. I want to find out . . .

FUMANI   Find out what?

JACOB   What kinds of things you do.

FUMANI   We struggle for better schools. But you told me you didn't want to have anything to do with us.

JACOB   I've changed my mind.

FUMANI   Oh, you have, huh? *(Beat)* How do I know you're not trying to infiltrate? How do I know you won't tell your teachers . . . or your father . . . or the police?

JACOB   I would never do that! *(Beat)* Not now, after what happened last week.

FUMANI   Well. *(Pause)* OK. There's a meeting in Durban Tuesday night. Let's start with that. *(Beat)* We can give you a ride.

JACOB   *(Beat)* OK. I'll come. But I want nothing to do with violence.

FUMANI   Neither do we, man. We're not **Umkhonto.** We don't train people to fight with guns.

(FUMANI exits.)

JACOB   *(To FRANKEL)* Later, that same man, his name was Fumani, recruited me into the African National Congress.

(The lights change. JACOB crosses downstage. FUMANI enters with a handful of leaflets and crosses to JACOB. The CHORUS enter upstage. It is two months later. We are in a field on the edge of Imbali.)

LEADER   **The mouth is still,**
But the blood will tell.

CHORUS   **The mouth is still,**
But the blood will tell.
(Repeat underneath.)

FUMANI   Here are the Freedom Charter leaflets I want you to hand out. (JACOB *reaches for the leaflets.* FUMANI *holds on to them.*) They'd send us to jail if they find us with these.

(FUMANI *lets go.* JACOB *starts to read a pamphlet.*)

JACOB   I'm not scared of them.

FUMANI   Good, don't be scared. But don't be stupid, either. *(Beat)* Have respect for the ideas on this piece of paper. Many of our people have *died* struggling for these ideas. I don't want you to be one of them.

JACOB   (*Reading the now familiar words with enthusiasm.*) We, the people of South Africa, declare for all our country and the whole world to know that South Africa belongs to all who live in it, black and white.

FUMANI   **Yebo.**

JACOB   All shall be equal before the law; all shall enjoy equal human rights! The doors of learning and culture shall be opened.

FUMANI   That one really speaks to you, doesn't it, **umfuwethu?**

JACOB   **Yebo.**

FUMANI   You know, we have a school up north.

JACOB   Where?

FUMANI   In Tanzania. Freedom College. Where our people get a real education.

JACOB   Do they teach about computers?

FUMANI   I'm sure they do. *(Beat)* Listen, you finish your studies here, OK? Learn as much as you can. Then maybe we can arrange to send you up north to Freedom College. Study computers. Later, you could come back and teach our people here.

JACOB **Yebo,** Fumani, **yebo.**

FUMANI **Yebo.**

(FUMANI *exits.* JACOB *is jubilant. The* CHORUS *cross downstage and circle the stage. The lights change. We are on a street in Imbali, later that afternoon.* JACOB *hands out leaflets to the* CHORUS. *The* LEADER *and two* CHORUS MEMBERS *cross downstage to sing.*)

CHORUS **The mouth is still, but the blood will tell.**

(*Repeat.*)

LEADER **We, the people of South Africa . . .**

CHORUS
MEMBERS
#1 AND #2
AND
LEADER
**Declare for our country
And the whole world to know,
That South Africa belongs
To all who live in it,
Black and white,
And that no government
Can justly claim authority
Unless it is based
On the will of the people.**

**The mouth is still,
But the blood will tell.**

(BEAUTY DLAMINI *enters. The* CHORUS *exit.* JACOB *stuffs the remaining leaflets in his shirt.*)

BEAUTY Jacob, where have you been?

JACOB Just . . .

BEAUTY What are you doing?

JACOB Oh, nothing.

BEAUTY Come on, the prayer service has started already.

JACOB It has?

BEAUTY **Yebo.** They said six, and it's already six-fifteen.

JACOB So we'll be there at six-thirty. We won't miss much.

BEAUTY *Only* the blessing and the testifying! I don't like to walk in late for that.

JACOB No one will notice.

BEAUTY You know how the **Umfundisi** feels.

JACOB You go ahead, then. I've got to finish something. I'll come right after.

BEAUTY Jacob! If you had something else to do, why didn't you tell me? **Ayi!** You've kept me waiting half an hour. You're always late these days. I should have gone ahead.

JACOB I'm sorry. Don't go, Beauty. I'm sorry.

BEAUTY No, I don't want to be late. *(Beat)* I know what you're doing.

JACOB What? *(Beat)* No, you don't.

BEAUTY Well, I know you're doing things for Congress. You have been for months now, haven't you?

JACOB Shh! **Thula!** [Quiet!]

BEAUTY Jacob, I don't understand how you can go with Congress and . . . and then say you're a Christian and lead the worship groups. Congress preaches hatred and violence and gets people angry and kills them and —

JACOB No, they don't! **Ayi!** The opposite! Beauty, does not the Bible command us to make this world a better place? Does it not?

BEAUTY Yes, but . . .

JACOB I'm just telling the masses the truth.

BEAUTY "Telling the masses the truth?" Oh, Jacob, you even talk like them now. *(Beat)* It's crazy. *(Beat)* I never get to see you anymore.

JACOB Well, then, give me a kiss.

BEAUTY Stop it. I'm serious. *(Beat)* You're deceiving your own father and mother.

JACOB No, I'm not. I'm . . . I'm protecting them. *(Beat)* They just don't understand.

(They kiss.)

JACOB And neither do you.

BEAUTY Well, I don't see how you can keep this up.

(BEAUTY exits.)

JACOB *(Calling after her)* You worry too much.

(FRANKEL enters stage left.)

FRANKEL Did you keep up your church activities?

JACOB Yes, I did.

FRANKEL And what did you do for the ANC?

JACOB Gave out leaflets, painted slogans on walls.

FRANKEL So, nothing violent?

JACOB No, nothing violent.

FRANKEL Now please tell the court what happened six months later.

(FRANKEL exits. JACOB crosses downstage. The lights change.)

Scene 12

It is October 1984. We are in the main room of the ZULU home in Imbali. MARTIN and REV. ZULU are at the table, MARTIN doing homework, REV. ZULU working on a sermon. JACOB stands fidgeting nervously. MRS. ZULU enters.

MRS. ZULU Dinner will be ready soon. Martin, put your things away.

MARTIN OK, Mama. I just want to finish this last problem.

JACOB Mama, what can I do?

MRS. ZULU *(In no hurry)* Well . . . you can set the table. Hezekaya, can you move your things?

(MRS. ZULU exits. REV. ZULU painstakingly starts to gather his books and papers. JACOB is in a great hurry, trying to move his father along.)

REV. ZULU Wait, wait, no. You're going to mix up all my pages here.

JACOB Sorry, **Baba,** sorry.

REV. ZULU I want to finish this tonight.

(JACOB tries to clear MARTIN's books and papers. MARTIN stops him.)

MARTIN Hey, man, cut it out. Trying to get out the door?

(JACOB shoots MARTIN a dirty look.)

(MRS. ZULU enters.)

MRS. ZULU Stop it, you two! *(Beat)* You want to go out again tonight?

JACOB **Yebo,** Mama.

REV. ZULU But you were out just last night.

JACOB I'm just going to study at Masizi's house. He's got books we use to study for the exams.

MARTIN Why can't you bring the books here?

JACOB **Wo, mfana!** [Hey, boy!]

MRS. ZULU Yes, why can't you?

JACOB Because, Mama . . . other people are coming, and we talk and discuss —

MARTIN Lots of things.

MRS. ZULU Martin! *(Beat)* Jacob, I don't like this. I want to talk with you.

JACOB Mama, I'm going to be late.

REV. ZULU Listen to your mother. Then we will sit down and have dinner as a family.

(From offstage, the SOUND *of a siren approaching.* MARTIN *goes to the window. Two uniformed armed* BLACK POLICEMEN *and* LIEUTENANT KRAMER, *a white plainclothes officer, enter upstage.)*

JACOB But, **Baba,** I'll be late.

REV. ZULU And then we will sit down to dinner as a family.

*(*MARTIN *turns to the others in horror.)*

MARTIN **Baba,** it's the police!

(The two POLICEMEN *and* LIEUTENANT KRAMER *burst into the* ZULU *home.* KRAMER *points to* JACOB.*)*

KRAMER **Daar is hy!** [There he is.]

(One POLICEMAN *grabs* JACOB, *crams his arms behind his back, pins him to the table, and handcuffs him. The other* POLICEMAN *crosses and exits stage right as if into a bedroom.* LIEUTENANT KRAMER *leafs through the papers on the table.* MARTIN *holds on to* MRS. ZULU.*)*

MRS. ZULU Jacob!

JACOB Hey! Let me go! Let me go!

REV. ZULU Stop that, stop that!

MRS. ZULU You're hurting him, you're hurting him!

MARTIN **Baba, Baba!**

(The first POLICEMAN *exits with* JACOB. *The other* POLICEMAN *returns with some leaflets, which he shows to* KRAMER.*)*

POLICEMAN   Lieutenant.

REV. ZULU   What is going on? What is going on?
(To KRAMER*)* Let him go. What . . . what . . . are you
doing to my son? Where are you taking him?!

MRS. ZULU   **Nkulunkulu wami!** [My God!]

REV. ZULU   What has he done?

*(*LIEUTENANT KRAMER *sweeps the papers from the table.)*

KRAMER   *(To the* POLICEMAN*)* **Kom, ons weg!** [Come on,
let's go.] *(To* REV. ZULU*)* Fuck off!

REV. ZULU   You can't just come in here and take him
away!

*(*LIEUTENANT KRAMER *and the* POLICEMAN *exit.* MRS. ZULU *is
hysterical.* MARTIN *and* REV. ZULU *try to comfort her. The*
CHORUS *enter, singing through the transition into the next scene.
They surround the* ZULU *family. Part of the* CHORUS *exit with*
MRS. ZULU *and* MARTIN. *The* LEADER *and* CHORUS MEMBER
#1 *cross the stage with* REV. ZULU.*)*

CHORUS   **Oh, Zulu, Zulu!**
          (Repeat for rest of song.)

LEADER   **Children of Heaven,**
AND   **You trusted to the Lord,**
MEMBER #1   **Prayed the Holy Shepherd**
            Watch over His flock.
            But the jackals have come
            And torn away the lamb.
            What will they do to Jacob?
            Beat him?
            What will they do to Jacob?
            Torture him?
            Torture him, torture him?

(The LEADER *and* CHORUS MEMBER #1 *exit. The lights change.)*

Scene 13

Interrogation room at a jail in Pietermaritzburg. There are two chairs and a table. It is three days later. Lieutenant Malan, *another white cop,* Lieutenant Kramer *and a* Black Police- man *enter with* Jacob, *whom they seat in a chair.* Rev. Zulu *enters.*

Malan   Ah, **Dominee** [Reverend]. Please come in. Sit down.

(Rev. Zulu *sits.)*

Rev. Zulu   Jacob, are you all right?

(Jacob *looks ahead in sullen silence.)*

Malan   **Ja,** he's fine. He's fine. We haven't touched him. Don't believe all that rubbish you hear. *(He con- sults a folder.)* Zulu . . . Hezekaya . . . Reverend, Imbali African Evangelical Church. *(Beat)* "Zulu." That means "heaven" in your language, doesn't it? Well, that's a good name for a minister, isn't it? *(Chuckles.)*

Rev. Zulu   Yes, sir, yes.

Malan   **Ja.** I'm Lieutenant Malan, Special Branch. And you've already met my colleague Lieutenant Kramer.

Rev. Zulu   Yes. Lieutenant, please, why is my —

Malan   **Ja,** I understand. Why is your son here? *(Beat)* **Meneer.** [Sir.] Your son is in very, very big trouble. I'm afraid we may have to keep him here for a very long time.

Rev. Zulu   Well, what . . . what has he done?

Malan   *(To* Jacob*)* Tell him. *(Pause)* Your son is a mem- ber of a banned organization. The African National Congress.

Rev. Zulu   What?

MALAN   He gave out this pamphlet to one of our undercover men. *(He hands* REV. ZULU *a mimeographed pamphlet.)* Go ahead, look at it. *(Beat)* This is what they call the Freedom Charter. Total, complete Communist propaganda. They want to tear down this country. *(He snatches back the pamphlet.)*

REV. ZULU   Did you do what the lieutenant says?

JACOB   *(Pause)* **Baba,** it's not what he says it is.

REV. ZULU   No, answer me. Did you?

JACOB   **Yebo, Baba,** but . . .

*(*REV. ZULU *is shocked.)*

KRAMER   Ask him how long he's been with the ANC, hey? Ask him. *For more than one bloody year!*

MALAN   *(Gesturing* KRAMER *to cool it.)* **Genoeg, genoeg.** [Enough, enough.]

REV. ZULU   Lieutenant Malan, I'm sorry. I don't know how this happened, but —

MALAN   **Meneer,** the law says your boy must go to prison for ten years.

REV. ZULU   No, no. Please, he's a very fine boy, he never makes trouble.

MALAN   I am sorry, but that is the law. You especially, **Meneer,** you must know that laws are made to be obeyed. How else can we tell what is right from what is wrong?

REV. ZULU   He didn't mean to hurt anyone. He's only a boy.

MALAN   *(Pause)* Well, I know how these organizations get their hooks into some kids who are basically good kids. *(Beat)* Listen. I'm willing to take a chance. To go out on a limb. We won't keep him.

Rev. Zulu **Dankie, Baas, dankie.** [Thank you, Master, thank you.]

Malan On one condition. *(To Jacob)* You cooperate with us. Give us . . . information.

Jacob Never!

(Lieutenant Kramer and the Policeman move menacingly toward Jacob. Malan gestures them back.)

Malan Look, I'm not fooling around now. You work with us, or you go straight to prison. That is your choice.

Rev. Zulu Lieutenant, may I speak to my son in private, please?

Lt. Malan *(Beat)* All right, **ja.** For a few minutes only. **Kom.**

(Malan, Kramer and the Policeman exit.)

Rev. Zulu Are you all right?

Jacob **Yebo.**

Rev. Zulu Did they hurt you?

Jacob *(Nodding)* They beat me on my chest and my back. I told them nothing, **Baba.**

Rev. Zulu I want you to do what the lieutenant asks.

Jacob No, **Baba!** I can't! You're asking me to inform on my comrades. *(Beat)* **Baba,** they will kill me.

Rev. Zulu Just tell him what he wants to know, so we can get out of here. *(Beat)* I warned you to stay away from those kids.

(Lieutenant Malan reenters.)

Malan So?

Rev. Zulu He . . . he will work with you, sir.

MALAN   Names, addresses, everything?

JACOB   *(Pause)* **Yebo.**

MALAN   No games, my boy. You play games with me, and I'll put you away for *twenty* years.

REV. ZULU   No, he'll do it, sir, he'll do it.

MALAN   Well, we'll see. He'd better. *(Beat)* Go. I won't press charges.

REV. ZULU   **Dankie, dankie.**

(LIEUTENANT MALAN and REV. ZULU exit. The lights change. We are on a street near Imbali High School. It is one week later. LIEUTENANT KRAMER and a BLACK POLICEMAN enter upstage. JACOB crosses upstage. They grab him. FUMANI and STUDENTS enter and cross downstage.)

KRAMER   **Kom japie** [Come on, dummy], that's enough. Which ones are your buddy boys? Hey? *(JACOB doesn't answer.)* Don't play the monkey with *me*, **bobbejaan** [baboon]. *(Beat)* Which ones are they?

(JACOB starts to lift his hand and point to FUMANI, then pulls it down. KRAMER signals to the POLICEMAN, who throws JACOB to the ground and twists his arm back.)

JACOB   Ow!

KRAMER   Aw, does that hurt, **bobbejaan?** Does it? *(He signals the POLICEMAN to twist harder.)*

JACOB   Stop, stop.

KRAMER   You think this is bad, hey, **bobbejaan** — you think this is bad? No, this is just the beginning. I'm still being nice. *(Beat)* Because *I* am the law out here, **kaffirjie** [little nigger]. *(He kicks JACOB.)* Tell me some fucking names! *(Pause)* **Laat hom gaan.** [Let him go.]

(JACOB gets up and starts to run off, but KRAMER trips him. He stands on JACOB's hand.)

JACOB   Ow!!

KRAMER We'll be back tomorrow. And the next day, and the next. However long it takes. So don't think you can trick me. You cannot. You are going to cooperate. **Ag ja,** we promised your father, didn't we?

(Two STUDENTS *enter and see* JACOB *with* LIEUTENANT KRAMER *and the* POLICEMAN. *The* STUDENTS *run off.* KRAMER *and the* POLICEMAN *exit.* JACOB *starts to run off, but the* CHORUS *enter, threatening him.)*

LEADER **We know who you are!**

CHORUS **We know who you are!**

    (Repeat, alternating with LEADER.*)*

LEADER **We saw that policeman with you.**
         The police have turned you, haven't they?
         We know who you are!

(The CHORUS *stamp their feet loudly and gesture at* JACOB *the same way they did at* MR. X.*)*

CHORUS **Impimpi! Umsheshelengwana! Informer!**

    (Repeat.)

(The CHORUS *cross upstage. The lights change.* JACOB *lies down and curls into a ball. It is very late at night, one week later. We are in the Zulu home. After a few seconds,* JACOB *starts moaning.)*

JACOB *(In his sleep)* No, no, no, no, no . . . don't, don't . . . let me go . . . *let me go* . . . stop . . . stop . . . *stop!* (JACOB *sits up, only half awake.)* Oh, God, no, no, *no!!*

*(REV. ZULU *enters in his undershirt and trousers.)*

REV. ZULU What's going on, what's going on? What's the matter?

JACOB *(Simultaneously)* Oh, my God, oh, God, please, God!

*(REV. ZULU *reaches for* JACOB, *but he pulls away.)*

REV. ZULU What's wrong, what's wrong?

JACOB I don't want to die, **Baba,** I don't want to die!

REV. ZULU You're not going to die, you're not going to die.

JACOB *Oh!* I've got to get away, I've got to get away! Oh, **Baba!**

REV. ZULU Where, where have you got to go? No, you don't.

(JACOB *clutches at* REV. ZULU.)

JACOB Don't leave me, **Baba,** don't leave me.

REV. ZULU I'm not going to leave you.

JACOB Please, stay here, stay here!

(JACOB *folds himself into his father's embrace.*)

REV. ZULU I'm right here, I'm right here. *(Pause)* It's those other kids, isn't it?

JACOB Oh, **Baba,** everything's such a mess, such a mess.

REV. ZULU It is them, isn't it?

JACOB Don't leave me, **Baba.**

(JACOB *hugs* REV. ZULU *tighter.* REV. ZULU *eases him down and covers him.*)

REV. ZULU You just rest. OK? I'm just going to get your mother. I'll be right back.

(JACOB *clutches at his father's arm.*)

JACOB **Baba,** I just want to be good, I don't want to be bad.

REV. ZULU You're not bad, you're good, you're good. I'll be right back.

(REV. ZULU *exits. The lights change.* FRANKEL *enters.*)

FRANKEL How long did this go on?

JACOB For nearly two weeks, and then my father told Lieutenant Malan. He sent us to a doctor, who gave me some tablets and an injection. *(Beat)* But I could not stay home anymore.

(JACOB *crosses the stage and picks up a telephone receiver from offstage, as* FRANKEL *exits.* JACOB *is now outside a store in Imbali. It is late October 1984.)*

JACOB Mama? No, no. I can't tell you where I am. Yes, I'm leaving. I just have to. I can't anymore. . . . Mama, don't . . . Please. *(Pause)* Hello, **Baba.** I'm sorry, I'm sorry. I can't tell you, **Baba.** I can't. Yes. No. No . . . I've got to. . . . I'll try to come back. . . . I will pray for you too. . . . No, I . . .

(JACOB *hangs up the phone and crosses the stage. He is unsure where to go.)*

CHORUS *(Barely audible whisper)* **Impimpi! Umsheshe-lengwana! Informer!**

(The CHORUS *harass* JACOB *as he crosses to them.)*

CHORUS *(Shouting)* **Impimpi! Umsheshelengwana! Informer!**

JACOB No! No!

(The lights change. The CHORUS *exit.)*

Scene 14

Later that same night, outside the house in Imbali where FUMANI *rents a room.*

JACOB *(Shouting)* Fumani! *Fumani!*

(FUMANI *enters.)*

FUMANI What the hell you doing? I told you never to come here.

JACOB I'm ready, **madoda.** I want to go.

FUMANI Go where?

JACOB Up north, to the school.

FUMANI No. I told you, we want you to stay *here*.

JACOB I *can't!* They'll kill me if I stay here.

FUMANI Who will kill you?

JACOB Everybody, man. *(Beat)* You know what's going on.

FUMANI *(Beat)* Well? **Impimpi?** Are you? Are you an informer?

JACOB No! No, I'm not, I'm not. It's the cops, man. They beat me, but I told them nothing.

FUMANI You told them nothing? Nothing at all?

JACOB Nothing. *(Beat)* Fumani, please.

FUMANI It's not easy, **mfana.** The border's very tight. Things are rough up there, very rough.

JACOB I don't care.

FUMANI Even if you're just a teacher. *(Beat)* And you won't be able to get back soon. Maybe never.

JACOB Fumani, I don't care. I cannot stay here. *(Beat)* Fumani. *(Beat)* I'm not an informer — oh, God, I'm not.

FUMANI Hey, I believe you. I believe you. *(He embraces* JACOB.*)* Did the cops follow you? Or any of the other comrades?

JACOB I don't know.

FUMANI You don't know?! **Ayi!** Are you out of your mind?!

JACOB I'm sorry. I was so —

FUMANI Man, you're getting us into big trouble!

JACOB Let's go, Fumani. Let's just go.

FUMANI *(Overlapping)* Shut up, will you? Just. . . .
thula! [be quiet!] *(Beat)* All right. You do exactly what
I tell you, understand? 'Cause if you don't, we could
both end up dead.

JACOB **Yebo.**

*(FUMANI crosses a few steps to check if there is anyone watching
or listening.)*

FUMANI *(Harsh whisper)* OK, let's go!

*(FUMANI exits. JACOB starts to follow, but the LEADER enters
and stops him with a gesture of his hand. The CHORUS enter.
JACOB falls to his knees in an attitude of prayer.)*

LEADER **Baba nomama,** [Oh, Papa and Mama,]

CHORUS **Baba nomama,** [Oh, Papa and Mama,]
Akusekho ukubuyela emuva.
[I've lost my way back to you.]
Kuphela nje khulekani.
[All that's left is prayer.]
Nami ngizokhuleka. [I will also pray.]
Usizi izinhlungu [My heart feels heavy]
Inhliziyo yami ithwelitshe.
[As if I were carrying a stone.]

LEADER **Pray for him.**

CHORUS **Pray for him.**

LEADER **I will pray for him.**
My heart feels heavy like a stone.

(JACOB exits.)

CHORUS **Fly away, fly away, pray for the boy Jacob!**
(Repeat.)

*(FUMANI and JACOB enter. They are fleeing to the Swaziland
border en route to Mozambique. They cross through the CHORUS
and exit.)*

Jacob, fly away, fly away.
(Repeat three times.)

LEADER **Pray for him, we will pray for him.
My heart feels heavy, like a stone.
There is no way back.**

(Lights fade to black.)

Act
T W O

Scene 1

The stage is clear. The LEADER *enters.*

LEADER   **Zithi nqonqonqo, zithi nqo!**
             [Knock, knock, knock, I'm knocking!]

(Repeat.)

(The LEADER *listens for a few seconds.)*

LEADER   **Wo ngaze ngahamba, ngahamba wema.**
             [I am wandering and roving all over.]

(The CHORUS *enter from all sides of the stage.)*

CHORUS   **Two shillings!**

LEADER   **Ngaze ngafik'esigodini Mozambique.**
             [I arrive in the valleys of Mozambique.]

CHORUS   **Two shillings!**

LEADER   **Bangibuza bathi mfan'ungubani?**
             [They ask, "What is your name, boy?"]

CHORUS   **Two shillings!**

LEADER   **Ngabatshela ngathi ngingu Jacob.**
             [I tell them, "My name is Jacob."]

CHORUS   **Two shillings!**

LEADER   **Bangibuza bathi mfana uphumaphi?**
             ["Where do you come from, boy?"]

CHORUS   **Two shillings!**

LEADER   **Ngabatshela ngathi ngiphuma Embali.**
             ["I come from the town of Imbali."]

CHORUS **Two shillings!**

LEADER **Awu yeni!** [Let us go!]

(FUMANI *and* JACOB *enter, run through the* CHORUS, *and exit.*)

CHORUS **Two shillings!**

LEADER **Wo ngaze ngahamba, ngahamba wema.**
[I am wandering and roving all over.]

CHORUS **Hide by day!**

LEADER **Ngaze ngafik'esigodini Mozambique.**
[I arrive in the valleys of Mozambique.]

CHORUS **Run at night!**

LEADER **Bangibuza bathi mfan'ungubani?**
[They ask, "What is your name, boy?"]

CHORUS **Fight to live!**

LEADER **Ngabatshela ngathi ngingu Jacob.**
[I tell them, "My name is Jacob."]

CHORUS **Live to fight! Fight to live! Live to fight!**

(*The* CHORUS *cross upstage and reveal* ZEBULUN, MBONGENI *and* PERCY, *black men in their twenties, sitting on crates and playing cards at a small table. There are two benches. We are in* MA BUTHELEZI's *two-room house in a black South African township near Piet Retief, close to the Swaziland border.* **Mbaqanga** [township] *music blares from the boom box on the floor. It is late in the evening at the end of October 1984.* MBONGENI *lays down his cards with a flourish.*)

PERCY **Ag, man, fock dit!** [Oh, man, fuck it!]

ZEBULUN Damn!

MBONGENI (*Raking in the money*) He, he, he! Come to **Baba,** come to **Baba!**

(MA BUTHELEZI, *a tired-looking older black woman with a blanket draped around her shoulders, enters with* FUMANI *and* JACOB.)

MA BUTHELEZI Zebulun, Zebulun. These two are here for you.

FUMANI **Sawubona,** Zebulun.

ZEBULUN Fumani! How's it, brother?
(They shake hands.)

FUMANI Good, good. *(Beat)* This is . . . Isithende. *(Beat)* Hey, man, we're going to his . . . his sister's wedding. *(Beat)* Can we spend the night?

PERCY **Herre man!** More people?

MA BUTHELEZI They have to pay. Two rand each.

ZEBULUN *(He digs for the coins.)* You going to be a rich lady one day, huh? *(He hands her two coins.)*

MA BUTHELEZI Don't be cheeky. *(She looks at the coins.)* This one can sleep in the front. The young one can stay here with Itshe. And no smoking **dagga** [marijuana] or bringing in women. I'm a Christian woman. *(She exits.)*

MBONGENI *(Yawns hugely.)* **Madoda,** that's it for me for tonight.
(He turns off the boom box. The music stops.)

PERCY Hey, **mfana,** where's your sister live? Where's the wedding? Huh?

JACOB It's . . . it's up north.

PERCY Well, shit, don't look so scared — you're not the one getting married!
(Laughter. MBONGENI and PERCY exit.)

ZEBULUN You want to take him across the border?

FUMANI **Yebo.** Soon as possible.

ZEBULUN OK. We'll leave tomorrow at dawn. *(Beat)* I need to talk to you. Outside.

FUMANI   Hey, is it safe to leave him here with this other guy?

ZEBULUN   **Ja, ja,** he'll be all right. Itshe keeps to himself. *(To* JACOB*)* Good night, my brother.

(ZEBULUN *exits.*)

FUMANI   Stay here, all right? Don't go anywhere else. Get some sleep; you will need it.

JACOB   OK.

FUMANI   **Lala kahle.** [Good night.]

JACOB   **Lala kahle.** *(Beat)* Fumani?

(FUMANI *exits.* JACOB *lights a candle on the table and sits down. After a few seconds,* ITSHE, *a black man in his early forties, enters. He's wearing a shabby raincoat. He stares at* JACOB *for a few more seconds, then crosses to the table.* JACOB *jumps up.*)

ITSHE   So . . . they put you in here, huh?

JACOB   **Yebo.** Just for tonight.

ITSHE   *(Pause)* What's your name?

JACOB   Isithende.

ITSHE   They call me Itshe.

JACOB   Itshe.

ITSHE   Where you from?

JACOB   South of here.

ITSHE   Where south?

JACOB   Near . . . near Pietermaritzburg, sort of.

ITSHE   Oh, a Maritzburg boy, huh? I used to ride the bus from Maritzburg to Durban. Through the Valley of a Thousand Hills. Beautiful. *(Beat)* "I will lift up mine eyes unto the hills from . . . from" . . . something, something, something, something.

JACOB "From whence cometh my help."

ITSHE Yeah, that's good. *(Laughs.)* That's good. *(Beat)* So. You're a Christian.

JACOB **Ja.**

ITSHE Good, good. Me, too. I'm Roman Catholic. *(Beat)* So what you doing way up here?

JACOB I'm going . . . I'm going to my sister's wedding.

ITSHE Your sister's wedding? *(Beat)* Where she live, in Mozambique?

JACOB *(Startled)* No, no; around here.

ITSHE Come on, man. You're not going to no wedding. You're going north, you're going to the camps. To join **Umkhonto. Ja, ja?**

JACOB No, I wouldn't do that.

ITSHE No? No? No?

JACOB No.

ITSHE You got a mother?

JACOB Yes, I have a mother.

ITSHE She loves you?

JACOB Yes, but . . .

ITSHE You got a father who loves you?

JACOB *(Beat)* Yes. What are you doing?

ITSHE Then go home! Go back. You'll never make it across the border. If you stay here, these **tsotsis** [thugs] here will eat you alive. And if they don't get you, the cops will.

JACOB I can take care of myself.

Itshe   Ha! Don't make me laugh. Take care of yourself? You'll end up dead or in prison. You ever been
to prison?

Jacob   **Ja,** I been to prison.

Itshe   Where, where?

Jacob   *(Beat)* It doesn't matter where.

Itshe   Come on, come on, tell me where.

Jacob   *(Beat)* Loop Street, Pietermaritzburg.

Itshe   Never heard of it. How long you there?

Jacob   Three days.

Itshe   Three days? Ha! Listen here, boy. You don't
know *nothing.* Three days? The first time I was in jail,
the *first* time, the fucking judge gave me two *months.* I
was *thirteen* years old. Can you cut cane sugar? Can
you break rocks with a hammer?

Jacob   No.

Itshe   That's not work for a child. *(Pause)* Your arms
swell up, they go numb, your hands bleed, your
fingernails rip off. You know how many fucking rocks
there are?

Jacob   No.

Itshe   The last time was eleven years, eleven years
hard labor. Wake up every morning, see some naked
guy shitting in a corner. One piss pot for fifty guys,
shit floating all over the place. The smell, the stink.
The screaming. The fighting five feet from your face.
At night it was worse. Men crying. *(Beat)* But those
white warders, man, you've never seen bastards like
that. They treated me worse than you would treat a
dog. You know how they count the prisoners? Make
you lie down on the floor and walk on your face with
their fucking boots. Two times a day for eleven years.

They put out their fucking cigarettes on your face, man — in your eyes, on your lips, in your ears! They kick your balls in! Every night I prayed, "God, take me out of this shit, just take me out of here!" Three times I tried to escape, three times those white bastards caught me, shoved me right into the fucking hole, right into the fucking hole. *(Beat)* Two times I tried to take my own life. *(Beat)* Don't tell me about fucking pain, man, you don't know shit about pain.

JACOB *(Pause)* I'm sorry.

ITSHE Sorry? Sorry? Don't you be fucking sorry for me! Because I know what I'm doing. God told me what to do. God sent me a dream.

(As ITSHE *speaks, his shadow is projected on the upstage wall. It grows in size until it becomes huge.)*

LEADER *(Under* ITSHE'S *speech)*
Wayinyathela wanyathela
[If you tread on the buck's tail]

CHORUS **Wayinyathela, Emsileni nyamazane?**
[How long before he turns on you?]

LEADER **Wanyathela?** [If you tread on it?]

CHORUS **Wayinyathela, kuyoze kube nini?**
[If you tread, how long will it be?]
(Repeat several times.)

ITSHE He told me He wanted me to be like Mgobhoze, Mgobhoze-over-the-mountain. He was fighting the enemies of Shaka. They had him pressed against the mountain and they were coming at him and he was stabbing, stabbing, stabbing and his arms were swelling up and his spear was slippery with all the blood and the blood was pouring down his body and . . . and the blood was rising up in my cell and I was going to drown in all the blood and . . . and . . . I had my hammer! I had my *hammer!*

71

(He swings the imaginary hammer. The CHORUS *chant changes to short percussive bursts that pick up the rhythm of* ITSHE's *words.)*

ITSHE   And I started to swing, swing, swing, kill, kill, kill . . . kill the white man, kill the white man, kill the white man! **Ngadla!!!** [I have eaten!!!] **Ngadla!!! Ngadla!!!**

(He stops. The CHORUS *stops chanting. The lights come up, and the huge shadow disappears.)*

ITSHE   *(Pause)* Go home. Go home to your mother, go home to your father, just go home. Let the other guys go to the camps. You go home.

JACOB   I'm not going to the camps. I'm going north to school. To become a teacher. Then I will come back and teach others.

ITSHE   No. You're not going to teach.

JACOB   What do you mean?

ITSHE   I can see it in your eyes. *(Beat)* You're going to have the same dreams and nightmares I have.

JACOB   You don't know what you're saying.

ITSHE   Maybe. Maybe I'm wrong. *(Beat)* Maybe it's too late already.

JACOB   You're crazy.

ITSHE   **Ja,** that's what the white man said. Crazy. *(Beat)* I'm going to sleep. You want the candle lit?

JACOB   No.

*(*ITSHE *blows out the candle, drapes his coat over* JACOB's *shoulders, crosses to a bench, and sits down. The lights change.* JACOB *sits brooding. The spotlight holds for several seconds. He gets up and paces in agitation.* LEADER *crosses downstage to the two figures.)*

LEADER   **It is dark in my mind,**
          It is dark in my heart.
          In my heart, I smell tear gas.
          It flows over my soul.
          Really this man is a messenger,
          Really this man is a messenger.

(ITSHE *gets up and stares at the* LEADER *for several seconds. The*
LEADER *retreats,* ITSHE *exits.* JACOB *gets up and starts to follow*
ITSHE, *but the* LEADER *stops him with a glance.* JACOB *sinks*
down on a bench.)

LEADER   **It is dark . . .**

CHORUS   **It is dark in my mind,**
          It is dark.

LEADER   **In my heart . . .**

CHORUS   **In my heart, I smell tear gas.**
          (Repeat three times.)

(FUMANI *enters and gestures for* JACOB *to follow. They exit. The*
lights change. The CHORUS *advance downstage.)*

LEADER   **Wo ngaze ngahamba, ngahamba wema.**
          [I am wandering and roving all over.]

CHORUS   **Two shillings!**

LEADER   **Ngaze ngafika ezitabeni Mozambique.**
          [I arrive in the valleys of Mozambique.]

CHORUS   **Two shillings!**

LEADER   **Bangibuza bathi mfan'ungubani?**
          [They ask, "What is your name, boy?"]

(*As the* CHORUS *continue singing,* JACOB *and* FUMANI *enter,*
running from a BORDER PATROL *offstage. We are on the South*
African / Swazi border later that night. There are muffled
SHOUTS, *the* SOUNDS *of engines revving and dogs barking. A*
follow spot plays over the stage, nearly catching them. JACOB *is*
distracted, immobilized. FUMANI *starts to dash off.* JACOB *doesn't*
move. The spotlight catches him for a second. FUMANI *sees him at*

the last minute, grabs him, shakes him and hauls him away from the light. They exit.)

LEADER   **Ngabatshela ngathi ngingu Jacob.**
[I tell them, "My name is Jacob."]

CHORUS   **Two shillings!**

LEADER   **Awu yeni.**
(Repeat.)

CHORUS   **Live to fight! Fight to live! Live to fight!**
(Repeat twice.)

(As the CHORUS *exit,* FUMANI *and* JACOB *enter.)*

Scene 2

A street in Matola, a suburb of Maputo, the capital of Mozambique, two days later. It is just before sunset in early November 1984.

FUMANI   *(Panting as he shouts.)* Michael? Ruth?

MICHAEL   *(Offstage)* Who's calling there, who's calling?
*(*RUTH DUBE, *an ANC guerrilla in her twenties, enters.)*

RUTH   Fumani? Is that you? Fumani!
(They hug.)

FUMANI   Ruth!

RUTH   You're OK, you're OK.

FUMANI   I'm fine, I'm fine.
*(*MICHAEL DUBE, *an ANC guerrilla in his twenties, enters.)*

MICHAEL   Fumani!

FUMANI   **Wethu!** [Brother!]
(They embrace.)

MICHAEL When did you get across the border?

FUMANI Just after dawn.

RUTH How was it?

FUMANI Rough. We ran into a patrol at Bothashoop.
We had to hide most of the night. *(Beat)* Comrades,
this is Isithende.

MICHAEL Welcome, Comrade! *(He shakes JACOB's hand.)*

RUTH Welcome to free Mozambique. *(She shakes JACOB's
hand.)*

FUMANI I'm taking him to Freedom College. He
wants to be a teacher.

MICHAEL Good, good, we need more teachers. *(Beat)*
We'll go into town first thing tomorrow and arrange
for transit.

RUTH It's going to take weeks, you know.

MICHAEL Hey, stay with us till you leave.

RUTH **Yebo,** we'll make room. Come in, come in.
Have something to eat. You must be tired.

FUMANI Thank you.

JACOB Thank you.

(FUMANI, RUTH and MICHAEL exit. FRANKEL enters.)

FRANKEL How long did you stay in Mozambique with
Michael and Ruth?

JACOB Nearly a month. We talked a lot about the
struggle. They showed me all the things that the
people had built in the town since the liberation: a
factory, a clinic, a day care center.

FRANKEL Yes. Now, back in South Africa around this
time, **Umkhonto we Sizwe** exploded a bomb outside a
South African Defense Forces headquarters.

JACOB Yes.

(MICHAEL *enters.*)

MICHAEL *(Shouting)* Ruth! Fumani! I think I hear something!

(RUTH *and* FUMANI *enter.* FRANKEL *exits.)*

FUMANI What is it?

MICHAEL Wait here. I'm going to see.

(*He exits.*)

JACOB What's going on?

RUTH Michael's worried the SADF will retaliate for the **Umkhonto** attack.

JACOB Here? Why here?!

(MICHAEL *enters.*)

MICHAEL Get down, everybody, *get down!*

(*They throw themselves down, just as the ROAR of airplane engines and the CHATTER of heavy machine guns sweep over the stage. A huge EXPLOSION follows.* RUTH *jumps up.)*

RUTH Michael! The children . . . !

(*She exits.*)

MICHAEL No, Ruth! Wait! Come back!

(FUMANI *starts to leave.*)

MICHAEL Don't go out!

FUMANI People may be hurt!

MICHAEL No. It's not safe yet! Come back!

(FUMANI *exits.* JACOB *starts to follow.* MICHAEL *restrains him.)*

You stay here! Stay here!

(MICHAEL *pushes* JACOB *down and exits. Again the ROAR of airplane engines overhead sweeps the stage, there is more GUN-*

FIRE *and an* EXPLOSION, *followed by* SILENCE *for several seconds. The lights go black. A spotlight picks up* JACOB. *He crosses upstage into a scene of carnage.* PEOPLE, *including* FUMANI *and* MICHAEL, *lie in various poses of death, reminiscent of the* VICTIMS *of the explosion at Shaka's Rock Mall.* FRANKEL *enters. The* CHORUS *enter and cross through the* VICTIMS, *who rise up to march in step behind the* CHORUS.)

CHORUS **Lalelani.**

> *(Repeat under dialogue.)*

FRANKEL Was anyone killed in this South African Air Force raid?

JACOB Yes. Seven people. *(Beat)* Two women who worked in the factory. A Cuban doctor at the clinic. Two children at the day care center. *(Beat)* Michael . . . and Fumani.

FRANKEL What effect did this raid have on you?

(Lights come up full. The CHORUS *and the* VICTIMS *now form a platoon of* **Umkhonto we Sizwe** GUERRILLAS. *They march in formation behind* JACOB.)*

JACOB It was on that day I decided to join **Umkhonto we Sizwe.** It seemed to me there was no other way to improve the life of the blacks in South Africa except through violence, to take up arms against the South African government. I went north to Angola, to the camps for military training.

Scene 3

October 1985. An **Umkhonto we Sizwe** *training camp in Angola.* JACOB *and the other* GUERRILLAS *march in place. They wear ragtag uniforms. Some cradle dummy AK-47 assault rifles. A huge blueprint of the inside of an AK-47 hangs above the stage. Downstage stands the* COMMISSAR, *a man in his mid-thirties, wearing snappy khaki combat fatigues and cradling a real AK-47.*

GUERRILLAS **Hamba kahle Umkhonto,**
[Fare you well, Spear,]
We Mkhonto, [You, Spear,]
Umkhonto we Sizwe.
[Spear of the Nation.]

(Repeat.)

COMMISSAR **Amandla!** [Power!]

GUERRILLAS **Ngawethu!** [Is ours!]

(Repeat twice.)

COMMISSAR **Take up your guns!**

GUERRILLAS **Hey, hey!**

(Repeat three times.)

COMMISSAR The oppressor has stolen our history, the true stories of the great heroes of all black South Africans! Xhosa, Sotho, Venda, Zulu. The Zulu emperor Shaka, who built a mighty nation and army in Zululand and who welcomed the white man, but they lied and tried to use him. **Viva** Shaka, **viva!**

GUERRILLAS **Viva!**

COMMISSAR Comrades, yesterday I talked about the rules of engagement. How is the African National Congress different from all other liberation movements? . . . We are the only liberation movement to sign the Geneva Convention. Don't forget that! *(Beat)* That means that we do not strike at civilians. Our targets are the oppressors' military forces, his economic forces, his police — and all collaborators, puppets, and informers. **Amandla!**

GUERRILLAS **Ngawethu!**

COMMISSAR Platoon . . . dismissed!

LEADER   **We are . . .**

GUERRILLAS   **We are the Spear,**
The Spear of the Nation.
We are the Young Lions —
Hear us roaring!
We will free you,
South Africa!
We will free you,
South Africa!

(The GUERRILLAS *begin to exit.)*

COMMISSAR   Comrade Isithende, wait!

*(*JACOB *crosses to the* COMMISSAR, *who looks around to make sure no one is listening.)*

COMMISSAR   Congratulations! We're sending you back in.

JACOB   You are? *(Beat)* I'm very happy.

COMMISSAR   **Yebo.** You've been here, what, nearly a year?

JACOB   Ten months.

COMMISSAR   So. I told them it was time to try you.

JACOB   Thank you, Comrade Commissar. *(Beat)* When am I to be sent?

COMMISSAR   Within a day or two.

JACOB   A day or two! *(Beat)* What will be my mission?

COMMISSAR   You'll be told at the proper time.

JACOB   Where am I to be sent, Com —

COMMISSAR   *(Interrupting)* At the proper time.

JACOB   I won't let **Umkhonto** down, Comrade.

COMMISSAR   No. *(Pause)* They're tightening up the border. Things have become much tougher inside South

Africa as well. Much tougher. Their **impimpis** and collaborators are everywhere.

JACOB   **Ja,** I know.

COMMISSAR   You know? Don't make me laugh. You know nothing.

JACOB   Well, that's what the others say.

COMMISSAR   The others! **Ayi,** they're even greener than you are.

JACOB   Yes, Comrade.

COMMISSAR   You know, of course, this will be your chance to end the rumors.

JACOB   I am aware of that. *(Beat)* I am not an informer. I am not! That's why I left!

COMMISSAR   Well . . . now you prove it.

JACOB   I will, Comrade. *(The* COMMISSAR *starts to exit.)* My mother and father. Could I . . .

COMMISSAR   No, absolutely not. If they know you are there, it could compromise the whole mission.

JACOB   Yes, Comrade.

(As the COMMISSAR *speaks, the lights change.)*

COMMISSAR   **Madoda,** I envy you. You get a chance to stick a knife in his belly. I tell you . . . I'm beginning to think like these youth over there.

(The COMMISSAR'S *following words are echoed on the loudspeaker by the* RADIO LIBERATION ANNOUNCER.*)*

COMMISSAR / RADIO LIBERATION ANNOUNCER   For too many years, too many years, only black families have wept at funerals. The white soldiers and police wage war on the black townships as if they were attacking another country, and then they return to the comfort and safety of their homes.

(*The* Commissar *exits.*)

Radio Liberation Announcer   (*Off, as if over a radio speaker*) We must destroy their sense of security. We must launch a people's war against the white soldiers and the police, in their barracks, in their homes, wherever they are, just as we have been attacking black collaborators and informers. The time has come when all of South Africa must weep! All South Africans, of every race, must feel that they are at war! **Amandla!**

(*The* Chorus *enter and physically pass* Jacob *over the border and back into South Africa. It is mid-November 1985.*)

LEADER   **Wo ngaze ngahamba, ngahamba wema.**
[I am wandering and roving all over.]

CHORUS   **Two shillings!**

LEADER   **Ngaze ngafik'emasimini South Africa.**
[I arrive in the fields of South Africa.]

CHORUS   **Two shillings!**

LEADER   **Bangibuza bathi mfan'ungubani?**
[They ask, "What is your name, boy?"]

CHORUS   **Two shillings!**

LEADER   **Ngabatshela ngathi ngingu Isithende.**
[I tell them, "My name is Isithende."]

CHORUS   **Two shillings!**

LEADER   **Bangibuza bathi mfana uphumaphi?**
["Where do you come from, boy?"]

CHORUS   **Two shillings!**

LEADER   **Ngabatshela ngathi amakamu Angola.**
["I come from the camps of Angola."]

(*The* Chorus *cross upstage.*)

Scene 4

The lights come up on the courtroom. It is the fifth day of the trial.

FRANKEL   When you arrived back in South Africa, where did you go?

JACOB   To a room in Edendale Township. Another comrade gave me money for rent and food.

FRANKEL   Who was this other comrade?

JACOB   My superior. He passed on instructions to me from the ANC.

FRANKEL   Whatever he said to do, you had to do it?

JACOB   Yes.

FRANKEL   What was your first assignment?

JACOB   To teach some people about firearms and explosives.

FRANKEL   Right. Now please tell His Lordship what happened on the evening of 20 December.

*(*JACOB *crosses downstage and lies down. We are in his rented room. The* SUPERIOR *enters and crosses to him.)*

SUPERIOR   *(Whispering)* Isithende! Isithende! Wake up, **madoda,** wake up!

JACOB   *(Rousing himself)* **Ayi, ayi!** What, what? Oh.

SUPERIOR   The Boers just attacked our people in Lesotho.

JACOB   *Lesotho?*

SUPERIOR   **Yebo.** They went in there with their airplanes. They killed nine of our brothers! Nine!

JACOB   Oh, **madoda.**

SUPERIOR   We've been ordered to retaliate. They want *you* to choose a target and hit it.

JACOB Me?!

SUPERIOR **Ja.** Hit it, **madoda,** *HIT IT!*

JACOB **Yebo.**

SUPERIOR You have four days: tomorrow, Sunday, Monday. By Tuesday at the *latest.* The people must see us retaliate for these attacks *straight* away. *(Beat)* Those are your orders. From the authorities. *(Beat)* **Sala kahle.** [Stay well.]

JACOB **Hamba kahle.** [Goodbye.]

(The SUPERIOR exits. JACOB returns to the dock. The lights change. We are back in the courtroom.)

FRANKEL Did he tell you how you were to retaliate?

JACOB No, but I knew he meant I had to hit someplace connected with the government or the police. The next day, I went to look for the target to hit.

FRANKEL Where did you go?

JACOB I went to Shaka's Rock, to the shopping mall. I saw the sign for South African Airways. To me, I always associated South African Airways with the government. I decided this is the place where I will retaliate.

FRANKEL But Shaka's Rock is a tiny resort town some sixty miles from where you were staying. Why did you not choose a target someplace closer, and in a city, like, say, Pietermaritzburg or Durban?

JACOB Too many people in those places know me.

FRANKEL Yes. Now were you personally in possession of any explosives or weapons of any kind?

JACOB No. I mean, that's why I approached Donald Thwala.

JUDGE Do not use that name!

JACOB Sorry, sorry.

FRANKEL Mr. X.

JACOB Yes, Mr. X.

FRANKEL Why did you place the bomb in a crowded shopping concourse, if you did not intend to injure innocent people?

JACOB Well, I was going to telephone a warning to the mall to get people out before the bomb goes off.

JUDGE For how long did you set the timer?

JACOB Thirty minutes.

FRANKEL What did you and Mr. X do after you set the limpet mine?

JACOB We separated, and I went to the post office to telephone.

FRANKEL Mr. X claims you were together. Mr. X never mentions a phone call.

JACOB He's lying.

FRANKEL Were you able to telephone?

JACOB No. I mean, all the telephones were being used. There was a queue for every phone. I could not possibly go up to people and say, "Excuse me, this is an emergency. Please may I phone?" I would have drawn attention to myself.

FRANKEL Yes. Did you see a telephone anywhere else?

JACOB No, I did not. I waited at the post office for ten minutes. Then I left. I decided that if I telephoned a warning now, there would be panic. A lot more people would be killed.

FRANKEL   Yes. What did you do then?

JACOB   I went home.

FRANKEL   Did you discuss the bombing with Mr. X later that day?

JACOB   No, I did not.

FRANKEL   Mr. X claims you were upset that only four people were killed. Mr. X says that you were unhappy that more whites did not die.

JACOB   He's lying.

FRANKEL   *(Beat)* Now, you were assaulted here by the father of one of the victims of this bombing. Why did you not press charges against him?

JACOB   To tell the truth, it relieved me when he struck me, because I am the cause of the death of his child. Pressing charges against him, that would just be another sin on me, really. *(Beat)* He loved his child, just like my mother and father love me. And I told my parents that they mustn't cry if they lose me.

FRANKEL   *(Beat)* If you had the opportunity again — if you were faced with this decision again — would you do it?

JACOB   *(Pause)* I would put the bomb elsewhere.

FRANKEL   No further questions, M'Lord.

JUDGE   Thank you. Mr. Dent?

(FRANKEL sits down. DENT crosses to JACOB.)

DENT   You would put your bomb elsewhere.

JACOB   Yes.

DENT   You said in your evidence that your enemies were the police, the army, and anyone connected with the government. Is that correct?

JACOB   Yes, sir.

DENT   So if it had been four *policemen* at Shaka's Rock, you wouldn't have *hesitated* in killing them?

JACOB   *(Pause)* No, I wouldn't. They oppress the people.

DENT   I see. *(Beat)* Now, the Accomplice has said that you expressed regret that only four people had been killed at Shaka's Rock.

JACOB   He's lying.

DENT   *He's* lying? *(Beat)* All right. Your training in Angola — it was hard?

JACOB   I was treated like a soldier.

DENT   "Like a soldier."

JACOB   Yes.

DENT   And you still regard yourself as a soldier of the ANC?

JACOB   Yes.

DENT   And not as some school child?

JACOB   No.

DENT   So what was your objective when you set out in the morning?

JACOB   I wanted to blow up the South African Airways office.

DENT   "Blow up the South African Airways office."

JACOB   Yes.

DENT   So in spite of your military training, you elected to put the limpet mine in an area crowded with civilians.

JACOB   *(Softly)* I thought I would avoid their death.

JUDGE I can't hear your answer.

JACOB I thought I would avoid harming the people by telephoning a warning to the mall.

DENT Well, how far was the post office from the Shaka's Rock Mall?

JACOB Five minutes walk.

DENT **Ja.** All right, now . . . once you realized that you wouldn't be able to telephone the mall, then you left to go home, not so?

JACOB Yes, I did.

DENT There were at least ten minutes left. You had time to go and remove that bomb from the mall. At your own risk. Why did you not?

JACOB Because, at that time, I did not think of going back to take the . . . the thing out.

DENT But you knew that people were going to die.

JACOB Yes, I did know.

DENT And you didn't do anything about it at that stage. Why not?

JUDGE *(Pause)* What is your answer?

JACOB I mean . . . it's just that if you would put yourself in my place, at that time, it would be something different.

DENT And why the daytime? Why set the bomb to explode in the daytime, when the shops were crowded with people? *(Pause) Why in the daytime,* Mr. Zulu? I'm still waiting for an answer.

FRANKEL With respect, M'Lord, the Accused is attempting to answer.

JUDGE Well, what is your answer?

JACOB   I mean, Shaka's Rock is a white area. A black man, myself, I would be arrested at night.

DENT   But why the shopping mall? Why not the post office, the police station, an electricity substation, the normal targets for these things?

JACOB   The police station and post office, I could not infiltrate those areas alone. I wanted to set the mine by myself. Donald Thwala just wanted to go with me, and I —

DENT   Please do not mention that name!

JUDGE   *(Beat)* When you gave your confession to the first magistrate, why did you not tell him about trying to warn the people?

JACOB   *(Pause)* Because I wanted to record that it is *myself* alone who did the crime.

JUDGE   I repeat my question: Why did you not tell him of your intention to telephone a warning so the police could clear the building in time?

JACOB   I . . . in fact, I . . . *(Pause)* I have no reason.

DENT   No further questions, M'Lord.

JUDGE   Thank you. Mr. Frankel?

FRANKEL   The Defense will call no further witnesses, M'Lord.

JUDGE   Very well. The Court will hear arguments on the subject of extenuating circumstances, and the closing statements, tomorrow morning.

(DENT and JACOB exit. The CHORUS cross downstage with FRANKEL.)

LEADER   **Ingane yeZulu!**

CHORUS   **Ingane yeZulu, Child of Heaven,**
Is Jacob this murderer
They say he is?
Let us hear from your mouth,
The kind of man that you are.

(*Repeat last two lines.*)

(*The lights change. It is the morning of the sixth day of the trial.*)

JUDGE   Mr. Frankel?

FRANKEL   M'Lord, we come now to the question of extenuating circumstances. Are there any factors which reduce the moral blameworthiness of the Accused? M'Lord, I believe there are. If we look at the overall picture of this young boy's life, M'Lord, we can see how he could end up doing something which would otherwise have been quite contrary to his Christian upbringing. Quite contrary to his very nature. (*Beat*) Unfortunately, M'Lord, this case encapsulates the tragedy of a whole generation of young black South Africans, that a young man, still in his teens, who has all the promise that his intelligence, his sensitivity and enthusiasm for life give him, is driven to leave his country and to take up arms against it. And ultimately to commit this terrible act. But it was not the act of a person driven by greed. It was not the act of a person who was self-seeking or who was robbing or stealing. Rather, it was the act, M'Lord, of someone who for that one moment of time lost all proper sense and judgment, one moment in an otherwise blameless life. It was the act of someone who was . . . *overwhelmed* . . . with frustration, with anger, with bitterness at the society in which he had grown up, a society torn apart by tensions, by conflicts, by . . . contradictions. Jacob Zulu is a victim of that society —

our society — and as a victim, he invites our com-
passion. *(Beat)* M'Lord, the State's primary witness,
Mr. X, is an accomplice turned informer. Experience
teaches us to suspect evidence from such a source.
The Accused has made it clear that he meant to harm
no one. His target was an agency he associated with
the government, not people. He has expressed regrets
and remorse for the unintended death and injury he
caused. *(Beat)* I submit that Your Lordship should not
think simply in terms of the retribution which society
may want to exact from this young man, but in much
broader terms. *(Beat)* With respect, M'Lord, is his
crime not a lesser one compared with the greater evil
of apartheid? Perhaps, to do this young man justice,
we would have to try not only his act, but the life and
the society that drove him to it. And in that sense,
M'Lord, we cannot judge Jacob Zulu. *(Beat)* But judge
we must. *(Beat)* The law may say that Jacob Zulu
should die. Justice . . . justice counsels that he must
live. *(Beat)* Thank you, M'Lord.

JUDGE   Thank you, Mr. Frankel. Mr. Dent?

DENT   M'Lord, we are not trying thousands of others
here today. We are trying *this* man, a trained soldier,
for *this* act, a terrorist atrocity. Why, if there are thousands of others like Jacob Zulu, why did *he* do what
he did? Why haven't all the others of his generation
done the same? It seems to me, M'Lord, my colleague
would offer the same defense no matter what young
black man were in the dock. By his line of reasoning,
if you are a black, then the state has no right to exe-
cute you no matter what your crime. If that is so, then
I shudder to think what this country will come to.
(Beat) No. We must see his actions for what they are.
The product of an evil mind. His was an attack
against society as a whole. Black and white, innocent
and guilty people. There could even have been other

members of the ANC present when the bomb exploded. And his was not a spur-of-the-moment decision. *(Beat)* What sort of person could walk into a shopping center carrying death in his hands and look into the faces of little children and go ahead and put death among them? *(Beat)* And, M'Lord, the picture of the Accused standing patiently at a telephone booth for ten or fifteen minutes and then simply shrugging his shoulders and deciding sort of "Oh, well," and off he goes: this behavior, if the story is even true, displays the most shocking, barbaric inhumanity. *(Beat)* The State requests the full penalty of death for these crimes.

JUDGE Thank you. I will endeavor to give judgment on this case sometime tomorrow morning. The Court will adjourn.

(The JUDGE, FRANKEL *and* DENT *exit. The lights fade to black.)*

Scene 5

The lights come up to half. It is later that same night in JACOB's *cell.* JACOB *is curled up downstage, asleep.*

LEADER *(Offstage)*
        Uyezwa uyezwa uyezwa na! [Do you hear, do you hear, do you hear that?]

        The CHORUS *enter upstage as* Zulu **impis** [regiments]. *They carry* **izihlangu** [large oxhide war shields] *and* **assegais** [stabbing spears] *and wear traditional headdresses and leggings.*

LEADER **We are coming,**
        Child of Heaven,
        We are coming!

CHORUS **Khuluma iqiniso!** [Tell the truth!]
        (Repeat several times.)

(CHORUS MEMBERS *dance in pairs and small groups all about the stage, eventually surrounding and waking up* JACOB. *The* LEADER *shouts the names of the different regiment each pair of warriors represents.*)

LEADER   **Khiphinkuzi!** [Drive the Bull from the Kraal!]
                Uphondo lwendlovu!
                [Horn of the Elephant!]
                Untaba yeZulu! [Mountain of Heaven!]
                Mkhuphulangwenu! [Lift the Crocodile!]
                Umanukelana! [Fight till the Blood Stinks!]

CHORUS   **Khuluma iqiniso!**

LEADER   (*Over the* CHORUS)
                **The warriors have gathered
                A council of elders.
                We're ready to listen.**

CHORUS   **The warriors have gathered
                A council of elders.
                We're ready to listen.**

LEADER   **Speak from your heart,
                Speak the truth.**

CHORUS   **Khuluma iqiniso!**

JACOB   You, **amaThongo,** you spirits of the fore-fathers, you come to me in my dreams. I tell you what I cannot tell my mother or my father. Or the lawyer. This is my story, **Nkosi.** (JACOB *gets up and paces around.*) **Umkhonto** sent me back to South Africa to a place near my home. My heart ached to see my parents and Martin. I feared I would come upon them by accident. I couldn't sleep. I was exhausted all the time. My nerves were stretched.

CHORUS   **Bayede Baba!** [Hail the father!]
                Bayede, bayede, bayede Nkosi!
                [Hail the king!]
                (*Repeat several times under* JACOB's *lines.*)

JACOB Up north in the camps, the instructors taught us to go out into the townships only at dawn, when the streets are full of people going to work. And just before dinner, when they come home. So that's when I went to train the others.

CHORUS **Be like the leopard**
Sliding through the bushes
Unseen, unheard, waiting to strike.

JACOB One day I thought I saw my girlfriend, Beauty, waiting in a taxi queue. **Madoda,** I thought my heart would leap out of my chest! I looked and looked, but it wasn't her. Another time, I was sure it was my parents and Martin. But it never was them.

CHORUS **Ntomb 'enhle kangaka** [You are a girl]
enje Ngobuhle belanga uma liphuma
lishona. [as beautiful as the sun rising and setting.]

LEADER **Khuluma iqiniso!**

JACOB When my superior told me to retaliate for the nine martyrs killed in Lesotho, I knew I had to prove myself. But where could I strike? Pietermaritzburg? Durban? No, too many people in those places know me. So I got a map and I looked on it. . . . and I saw it. **Itshe likaShaka,** Shaka's Rock. Where the Zulu regiments fought the enemies of Shaka. I must strike someplace *there.*

LEADER **Bayede!**

CHORUS **Sikidi!** [Finish them off!]

LEADER **Bayede Baba!**

CHORUS **Bayede, bayede, bayede Nkosi!**
(*Repeat under* LEADER *and* JACOB.)

LEADER **When Shaka, the great king of the Zulus,
Wanted to kill his enemies . . .**

CHORUS **When Shaka, the great king of the Zulus,
Wanted to kill his enemies . . .**

(The LEADER *passes his* **assegai** *to* JACOB.*)*

JACOB When Shaka, the great king of the Zulus,
wanted to kill his enemies, he sent his **impis** to catch
them up like the horns of the buffalo. They took them
high on the rock and drove them down into the sea.

(The CHORUS *thrust with their spears, then raise them.)*

CHORUS **Ngadla, ngadla!** [I have eaten!]

JACOB I took a bus to Shaka's Rock. I had never been
there before. It was full of white people. I had not
seen so many white people in years. They scared me.
(Beat) Then I saw the rock and the waves pounding
below it. **Madoda!** What have these white people
done to it? They put their stinking little shops around
it! This is what they do to our history?! *(Beat)* And
when I looked at the white children, I swear, all I
could see in my mind were the little black babies
killed in the air raid in Mozambique. And when I saw
their parents, I saw the white pilots in their airplanes
and the fascist police who tortured me. I looked at the
white youth and I could see the white minister's kid
laughing at me. I saw the cops who gassed us and
beat us. They have taken my family from me, they
have taken my dreams from me and . . . my life from
me! *(Beat)* And my deadline was coming up! I didn't
know what to do. I had such a fire in my chest, I
couldn't breathe. *(Beat)* And I went into the Shaka's
Rock Shopping Mall and I saw the sign for the South
African Airways and I heard in my head what they
said to us up north, they said you must bring the war
into *every* white home in South Africa. But they also

said, they also said, you must not harm civilians! And
I didn't know what to do! So I left the mall and I
went to the post office, but the police were checking
people there for their passbooks. It was getting dark.
Still I had no target, and time was running out.

(JACOB *crosses upstage as the* CHORUS, *dividing into two groups,*
sweep to the sides of the stage, driving away imaginary enemies
with shields and spears. They make the sucking sound of spears
being pulled from bodies.)

CHORUS **Shu, shu, ixwa, shu, shu, ixwa!**

(REV. ZULU, MRS. ZULU *and* PHILIP, JACOB's *older brother,*
enter upstage. PHILIP *lies under a blanket.* REV. ZULU *and* MRS.
ZULU *kneel next to him.* MARTIN *enters upstage and lies down.*
JACOB *kneels next to him. The drone of an* **ugubu,** *the traditional*
Zulu bow, is heard faintly offstage. JACOB *is remembering a night*
at the Zulu home in August 1976.)

CHORUS (*Coughing and wheezing in slow rhythm*)

JACOB That night, I dreamed of my brother Philip.
His coughing woke me up. He was in my parents'
bed. They'd hung a blanket around it. Light was coming through on the sides of the blanket. I sat up in
bed. Martin was still sleeping. I remember the bed
feeling so warm and Martin's legs on mine. My father
was praying. My mother was crying. I knew something was very wrong. "Mama? Mama?" (*Pause.* MRS.
ZULU *does not answer.*) She did not answer. I lay there
listening for a long time. Sometimes my mother
stopped crying and prayed with my father. Then
she'd start crying again. I was so scared. Finally, I fell
asleep. The ambulance woke me up. My father went
with Philip to hospital, while my mother stayed with
Martin and me. But it was too late. (*He crosses down-*
stage. The ZULU *family exit. The* CHORUS *cross downstage.*)
You see, we had been waiting for that ambulance for
hours. And I knew if Philip had been a white
boy . . . that ambulance would have come in time.

(Pause. The SHOPPERS *and* WORKERS *at Shaka's Rock Mall enter upstage and cross about. The Zulu bow is replaced by tinny Christmas carols playing over a loudspeaker.)*

So the next morning, when I woke up, I knew what to do. I had chosen my target. I found Donald Thwala, he fetched the mine, and we went to Shaka's Rock Mall. *(Beat)* And it was almost beautiful. That mine slid from my hand and landed . . . so . . . almost without a sound. And I knew that the dustbin would explode into a thousand pieces and the windows would shatter and slice like knives. . . . And my heart began to beat . . . like a *hammer!* And God, I was happy! And Donald and I walked *straight* to a taxi, and I went *straight* to my room. And that afternoon I read that four had died.

*(*JACOB *swings an imaginary hammer. There is an enormous* EXPLOSION. *All the* SHOPPERS *and* WORKERS *collapse.)*

And I wanted more. I wanted white people to die. *(He weeps.)* Oh, God, forgive me, for I have sinned! *(Beat)* I have shamed my parents, I have shamed the ANC! Oh, God, forgive me! *(Beat)* When the police came for me, when the police came, I wanted them to kill me. I wanted to die. And I didn't tell them about Donald because only Donald knew I had wanted to kill *people!* *(Beat)* And God, then I saw my parents and . . . and it was for *their* sake and to make good the wrong I had done to the name of the ANC that I made up the story about the phone call! *(Beat)* Oh, God, please forgive me! Forgive me! *(Pause)* So be it.

(The LEADER *crosses to* JACOB *and eases him back to sleep.)*

LEADER **Jacob, Jacob . . .**

CHORUS **Child of Heaven,**
You must be strong now.
The war is not over.
(Pause)

LEADER **We are coming,
Child of Heaven,
We are coming.**

CHORUS **Khuluma iqiniso, khuluma iqiniso!**

(Repeat six times.)

(The CHORUS *cross upstage. The* SHOPPERS *rise up as the*
CHORUS *approaches and exit with them.* JACOB *sleeps downstage.*
Slowly, the lights fade to black.)

Scene 6

The courtroom, the morning of the seventh day of the trial.

JUDGE The evidence against the Accused may be sum-
marized as follows: his confession and the testimony
of the Accomplice. *(Beat)* It is clear that the Accused
caused the Accomplice to obtain a limpet mine, that
the Accused placed it at Shaka's Rock Mall and that
the Accused detonated it. *(Beat)* It is therefore estab-
lished beyond all question in the judgment of this
Court that the Accused is *guilty as charged on all four
counts of murder. (Pause)* Now, the Accused maintains
he did not intend to kill people and that he tried to
issue a warning to Shaka's Rock Mall, so that it could
be evacuated. The Accomplice testified that this was a
deliberate, premeditated killing. *(Beat)* I am firmly of
the opinion that the Accomplice spoke the truth. The
Accused's story about trying to telephone a warning
from the post office is preposterous. He was evasive
in his replies. *(Beat)* I have also given full care and attention to the fact that the Accused is a young man.
(Beat) But the factor which has weighed most heavily
with me is that his was a deliberate, indiscriminate
attack on the innocent civilian population. *(Beat)* It is,

therefore, this Court's judgment that extenuating circumstances that would lessen the moral blameworthiness of the Accused are not present in this case.

DENT   M'Lord, purely for completeness of the record, I indicate that the Accused has no previous convictions.

JUDGE   Is there anything you wish to say, Mr. Frankel, at this stage?

FRANKEL   *(Beat)* No, M'Lord. There is nothing more that I can say.

JUDGE   Jacob Themba Zulu. You have been found guilty on four counts of murder without extenuating circumstances. Is there anything you wish to say before I pass sentence upon you?

JACOB   Yes. I wish to say first that the ANC never gave me instructions to kill innocent people. And I'd like to say to those people who lost their family members because of what I did, I am sorry. If I could give part of my flesh to those who remain, I would do it gladly. *(Beat)* And I hope the South African Defense Forces do not retaliate for these deaths by attacking neighboring countries.

JUDGE   *(Beat)* Yes. Thank you.

JACOB   And . . . and whilst in prison, my father and I . . . my father and my mother . . . we have talked. They know that I must die for what I did. But God will forgive me. And I am not sad, really, because my soul is going to glory. Soon I will see my brother Philip. *(Pause)* You see, people die all the time. Even when their breath does not stop, they die inside their heart. *(Beat)* And I hope that my life is a lesson to my brother Martin and to all the youth. *(Pause)* That is what I wish to say.

JUDGE Thank you. *(Beat)* On Count One you are sentenced to death. On Count Two you are sentenced to death. On Count Three you are sentenced to death. And on Court Four you are sentenced to death. May the Lord have mercy upon your soul.

(After the JUDGE's pronouncement of the sentence on Count Two, the CHORUS enter singing from the rear of the theater and make their way down the aisles to the stage. They are taking the last walk of condemned prisoners to the gallows in Pretoria Central Prison. It is April 29, 1986. The CHORUS sing through the JUDGE's sentencing and continue singing after the JUDGE finishes. As they sing, the GUARDS exit and reenter upstage pushing a gallows onstage. JACOB crosses to the gallows stairs. A GUARD fixes shackles on his wrists. JACOB climbs the stairs. The GUARD fixes the noose around his neck.)

LEADER **Wozani! [Come!]**

CHORUS **Wozani sihambe**
Siyezulwini
Siyobona amanxeba
Ezandleni zakhe

(Repeat the above two or three times.)

Ocelayo uyaphiwa
Ofunayo uyafumana
Ongqongqothayo uyavulelwa
Nqeqama leNkosi

(Repeat the above.)

Ninqakhali bazalwana bami
Sahlukene umzuzwa nje
Ezulwini sobonana futhi
Zonki nsizi seziphele nya.

[Come see the wounds of Christ in Heaven,
Ask and ye shall receive,
Seek and ye shall find.
Knock on the gates of Heaven,
And they will welcome you.
Don't cry, my brethren,
We part for only a short while.

In Heaven, we will see each other again.
There will be no sorrow.]

(The Protestant hymn **"Rock of Ages"** *may be substituted for the above.)*

JUDGE   The Court will rise.

*(*JACOB *raises his shackled hands in a salute.)*

JACOB   **Amandla!**

(Blackout. There is the sound of the gallows trap swinging open. Silence for a few seconds. The lights come up on the LEADER. *The gallows are empty.)*

LEADER   **The fire is burning,**
           It lights up the sky.
           From high on the rock,
           Down to the sea.

CHORUS   **Lalelani, lalelani.**

           (Repeat.)

(The lights come up full. The entire cast join the CHORUS *in singing.)*

LEADER   **This is the song of a young man**
           Called Jacob Zulu,
           Who suffered for the sins of South Africa.
           This is the song of those for whom
           The good news of the end of apartheid
           Comes too late.

CHORUS   **Amen.**

LEADER   **Too late.**

CHORUS   **Hallelujah.**

(The lights fade to black.)

After the curtain call, the whole ensemble sing the South

African liberation anthem, "**Nkosi Sikelel' iAfrika**"
[God Bless Africa].

Nkosi sikelel' iAfrika
Maluphakanyisw' uphondo lwayo
Yizwa imithandazo yethu
Nkosi sikelela
Thina lusapho lwayo.

(Repeat all the above.)

Woza moya, woza!
Nkosi sikelela, Nkosi sikelela!
Woza moya, woza!
Woza moya oyingcwele
Nkosi sikelela
Thina lusapho lwayo.

Morena boloka
Sechaba sa heso
O fedise dintwa le Matsoenyeho.

O se boloke, O se boloke,
O se boloke, Morena,
O se boloke.
Sechaba sa heso
Sechaba sa Afrika
Makube njalo,
Makube njalo.

Kuze kube nguna phakade
Kuze kube nguna phakade.

[God bless Africa,
Raise its banner high.
Hear our prayers.
God bless us, Thy children.

(Repeat all the above.)

Come, Spirit, come!
Come, Spirit, come!
Come, Holy Spirit!
God bless us, Thy children.
Save our nation,
End the war and misery.
Save us, O Lord,
Save our nation,
The nation of Africa.
Let it be so
Forever and ever.]

Lyric and Music Credits

Lyrics appearing on pp. 5–6, 8–9, 10, 12 (top), 17, 22, 25 (top), 26–27, 32, 33, 34, 37–38, 54, 59, 77, 79, 89, 91, 92, 93 (top and bottom), 94, 96, 100, by Tug Yourgrau

Lyrics appearing on pp. 12 (bottom), 16–17 (top), 19, 25 (bottom), 39, 47, 49 (top), 71, 73 (top), 93 (middle), 99, by Ladysmith Black Mambazo

Lyrics appearing on pp. 14, 15, 42, 44, 49 (bottom), 78, 99, from traditional songs or in public domain

Lyrics appearing on pp. 63–64, 65–66, 73 (bottom), 74, 81, by Ladysmith Black Mambazo and Tug Yourgrau

All music composed and copyright © 1993 by Ladysmith Black Mambazo with the exception of traditional songs appearing on pp. 14, 15, 42, 43, 44, 78 (top), now in public domain.

"Nkosi Sikelel' iAfrika," by Enoch Sontonga, 1897. Translated by Rev. Philip Ntombela and Tug Yourgrau.

Acknowledgments

I want to acknowledge the help of many others in creating *The Song of Jacob Zulu*: The Steppenwolf Theatre Company, Stephen Eich, managing director, Randall Arney, artistic director, for commissioning and mounting the play; Carmel Rickard and Paddy Carney, for their thoughtful and generous assistance; Reverend Philip Ntombela of the Parish of All Saints, Gingindlovu, South Africa, who, during his year at the Harvard Divinity School, helped with translations and gave me the gift of his friendship and insight; Peter Cook of WGBH, for his enduring enthusiasm and keen editing skills; Denis Kuny, Esq., the chief defense attorney at Andrew Zondo's trial, who provided valuable background information, and whose oratory on behalf of his client remains intact in several portions of the play; Professor Lynn Berat of Yale University's Southern African Research Program, Professor Helen Kivnick of the University of Minnesota and Lawyers for Human Rights, Durban, for their assistance; Mdletshe (Albert) Mazibuko and Madoda (Russel) Mthembu, both of Ladysmith Black Mambazo, Simpiwe Duma, Professor Elkin Sithole of Northeastern Illinois University, and Professor Susan Booysen of Rand Afrikaans University, for translations; Ladysmith Black Mambazo's business manager, Mark Silag, and their one-time tour manager, Mitch Goldman, for their commitment to the play; my agent Peregrine Whittlesey, for her hard work on my behalf; and Jack, Lois, and John Ahrens, Tracy and Blair Baker, Kim and Paul Mayer, Joel Olicker, and Barry Yourgrau for their continued encouragement and support.

My deepest gratitude goes to my wife, Beth, for her

loving steadfastness and buoyant optimism in the face of the mighty swings of the author's mood as he worked on the play and the play worked on him; for keeping our home on a more-or-less even keel during my frequent absences; and for her valuable insight into each new scene as it came off the printer.